GROUNDWORK GUIDES

Series Editor
Jane Springer

GROUNDWORK GUIDES

Technology
Wayne Grady

Groundwood Books
House of Anansi Press

Toronto Berkeley

Groundwood Books / House of Anansi Press
110 Spadina Avenue, Suite 801, Toronto, Ontario M5V 2K4
or c/o Publishers Group West
1700 Fourth Street, Berkeley, CA 94710

We acknowledge for their financial support of our publishing
program the Canada Council for the Arts, the Government of Canada through
the Canada Book Fund (CBF) and the Ontario Arts Council.

 Canada Council   Conseil des Arts   ONTARIO ARTS COUNCIL
for the Arts   du Canada   CONSEIL DES ARTS DE L'ONTARIO

Library and Archives Canada Cataloguing in Publication
Grady, Wayne
Technology / Wayne Grady.
(Groundwork guides)
ISBN 978-0-88899-982-5 (bound).—ISBN 978-0-88899-984-9 (pbk.)
1. Technology—History. 2. Technology and civilization. 3. Technology—Social
aspects. I. Title. II. Series: Groundwork guides
CB478.G73 2010   303.48'3   C2010-902463-X

Design by Michael Solomon
Typesetting by Sari Naworynski
Index by Gillian Watts

Mixed Sources
Product group from well-managed
forests, controlled sources and
recycled wood or fiber
www.fsc.org Cert no. SW-COC-001352
© 1996 Forest Stewardship Council

Printed and bound in Canada

Contents

For Merilyn.

Chapter 1
Technology and Us

I remember when Hurricane Katrina struck the south-east coast of the United States in September 2005. The high winds and flooding killed more than 1,800 people and caused such enormous damage that the city of New Orleans is still recovering from it. Powerful waves also destroyed thirty oil-drilling rigs in the Gulf of Mexico, and disrupted the flow of oil from offshore wells to refineries on the mainland. The resulting oil shortage exacerbated the public unease caused by the storm. In response, then president George W. Bush appeared on television and urged everyone to use less oil until the pipelines could be repaired.

"Don't worry," the president told the people. "Technology will find a solution."[1]

Two things about Bush's statement struck me as odd. One was the way he referred to technology as an entity somehow separate from human endeavor. He did not say that human beings — technicians, engineers or oil company executives — would get the US out of its predicament. Something called "technology" would.

The second, related to the first, was the implication that, having turned technology into an independent entity, we were relying on it to get us out of trouble. We have handed responsibility for our salvation over to this thing called technology. In other words, we were not in control of the rescue operation, technology was.

When critics of technology argue that human beings have become "slaves of the machine," they mean that we have assigned to this process called technology the power to dictate and control our actions. Like worker ants in a gigantic ant colony, we unthinkingly carry out functions assigned to us by a distant and abstract authority.

It hasn't always been that way. In fact, technology began as a means of bending nature to our will. At the close of the Pleistocene Era, roughly 10,000 years ago, when the end of the last Ice Age permitted the rapid growth of agriculture, humans developed a primitive form of farming that did not require tools. It wasn't until about 3,000 years later that implements such as axes and plows were developed as means of making it easier to work the land. At that time, we still controlled technology, which in turn allowed us to control our environment.

At some point in our history, however, we relinquished control of technology. By becoming reliant upon machines and the systems that support them for our survival, we became more attuned to their needs than to our own. In fact, their needs *became* our needs. For example, as human beings, we don't need oil: machines need oil. But since we believe that we need machines, we have come to believe that we need oil.

When did this change in our relationship with technology occur? And why? What are the consequences for our relationship with ourselves, our environment and our future? Before we can address any of these questions, we need to have a clear understanding of what technology is.

Let's start with what it is not. First, it is not simple tool use. Many animals use tools. For example, woodpecker finches on the Galapagos Islands use cactus spines and even wood chips to pry insect larvae from the bark of trees. Dolphins off the coast of western Australia have been observed protecting their faces with marine sponges while probing the sea floor for stonefish, whose sharp spines can deliver a severe shock. Great apes in the Congo use stones to crack nuts, and Egyptian vultures in Tanzania use stones to open hard-shelled ostrich eggs.

And although *Homo sapiens* ("the Wise") has been referred to as *Homo faber* ("the Maker"), technology is more than the ability to manufacture tools. New Caledonian crows routinely clip, peel, strip and split screw-pine leaves to make hooked tools for extracting insect grubs from the ground. And in an experiment conducted at Oxford University, a female New Caledonian crow actually bent a length of wire into a hook and used it to lift a small bucket of food from a vertical standpipe.

Technology is more a process than a thing. It is, as economist C.E. Ayres wrote in 1944, "simply organized skill."[2] It is the word "organized" that is important here. Neanderthals (*Homo sapiens neanderthalensis*), our ancestors in the evolutionary chain that runs from tool-using apes to us, lived from 250,000 years ago to about 24,000 years ago. They used simple stone tools, known as "flakes," for butchering meat and scraping skins. They also used spears, although for thrusting, not throwing. These tools show up in the most recent Neanderthal archaeological sites, suggesting they may have learned tool use from our more direct ancestors, the technically sophisticated Cro-Magnons, who migrated into Europe from Africa around that time.

Cro-Magnons were more "organized" than Neanderthals. They, too, used stone tools for cutting and scraping, but their stone blades were attached to handles in what can be seen as a rudimentary manufacturing process. They also made implements from a wider variety of materials, including bone, antler and ivory. They used tools for piercing and chiseling as well as for pounding and cutting, and they threw their spears, which meant they could kill their prey from a safe distance. Graeme Gibson suggests that this was the beginning of our separation from nature.[3] Organized tool use was certainly the start of our idea that nature was something we could control.

Tool use allowed Cro-Magnons to make fire, and thereby keep warm and protect family groups from predators. (Neanderthals had been mostly solitary, not living or traveling in family groups.) With tools they fashioned clothing and shelter, allowing them to inhabit areas that would otherwise have been unsuitable. These activities constituted a social structure. For example, techniques for making axes had not only to be developed, but remembered and passed on from one person to another, and from generation to generation. Toolmaking became a craft, or a trade, and so represented a new way of thinking about the environment. Cro-Magnons knew which aspects of their surroundings were permanent, which could be altered by hand, which required tools, and which tools were needed to make more tools. This is what is meant by "organized skill." With organized skill, Cro-Magnons were able to manipulate their environment rather than let nature manipulate them. It is *Homo faber* combined with *Homo sapiens*: human beings as both makers and thinkers.

Technology, then, is a way of thinking about a problem, and a way of putting thought into practice. It is therefore a series of actions, or techniques. "Technology is not the sum of the artifacts, of the wheels and gears, of the rails and electronic transmitters," writes Canadian physicist Ursula M. Franklin. "Technology is a system. It entails far more than its individual material components. Technology involves organization, procedures, symbols, new words, equations, and, most of all, a mindset."[4]

When we use a shovel to make a road, we are using technology in probably no more sophisticated a way than when a great ape uses a stick to extract honey from a hollow tree. But when we design a network of roads into towns, and organize the people living in those towns so that they make the most efficient use of the roads, then we are not only using technology, we are thinking technologically. In a way, roads became inevitable once we had created the wheel.

The wheel was invented in about 3500 BC, probably in Mesopotamia, as a way of increasing the output of clay pots: the first wheel was a potter's wheel. It made work easier and faster and therefore more efficient. Civilization has benefited from the wheel, whether it is attached to a barrow or a mill or an automobile. Complex machines like mills and automobiles have given us a wealth of vital products and have raised our standard of living as well as our level of health. But at the same time, they have changed the way we think. Whatever else we think of the wheel and its derivatives, solving a problem by inventing the wheel was an example of technological thinking; it was to set off down a road that began as a footpath and ends as a runway. In general, technology, like evolution, is irreversible and does not become simpler but ever more complex. The philosopher Henri Bergson suggested as much by defining human intelligence as "the faculty to create artificial objects, in particular tools to make tools, and to indefinitely vary its makings."[5]

The wheel, whether applied to pottery or to transportation, introduced to the world the notion of speed. Within the technological mindset, speed is all important: it represents efficiency, which is another way of saying profit. In manufacturing, speed means more goods delivered more quickly and sold in greater quantities.

In philosophical terms, speed is the conquest of time and space. Almost every new technology has been prized because it is faster than its predecessor. The cart was an improvement on the sledge because it was faster. Each new generation of laptop computer, or new version of Microsoft Word, must be milliseconds faster, and therefore "better," than the previous version. Each new printer must print more pages per minute than its predecessor.

The American architect Buckminster Fuller illustrated the shrinkage of time and space as a result of technological advances by representing the portion of a person's life taken up by traveling for a certain distance as a sphere. When the person walked, the sphere's diameter was seven meters (twenty-three feet). When the same person traveled by horse, the sphere's diameter was reduced to two meters (seven feet). With sailing ships, the sphere became a basketball; with the railroad, a baseball; and so on until, with modern jet travel, the sphere practically disappears altogether.[6]

To Lewis Mumford, such a reduction, far from representing progress, is actually a retrogression in human development. "Plainly," he writes, "the effect of speeding transportation is to diminish the possibilities of direct human experience." A person who walked or even rode a horse or a bicycle around the world "would have stored up rich memories of its geographic, climatic, esthetic, and human realities." The person would have become a more fully realized human being. One who flies around the world on a supersonic jet has, by comparison, "no experience at all."[7] Speed emphasizes quantity over quality. A student who copies out a poem of Margaret Atwood's by hand for a term paper knows something of the poem when he or she has finished; someone who cuts and pastes the same poem from a poetry website can do so more quickly and efficiently, but without knowing or learning anything about the poem.

"It is the Age of Machinery," Thomas Carlyle declared in 1829, in the aftermath of the Industrial Revolution. Carlyle viewed the increasing mechanization of Europe with a jaundiced eye. "Our old modes of exertion are all discredited, thrown aside,"[8] in favor of a system that valued only calculations of profit and loss. By a few decades into the nineteenth century, we had become slaves to the machine — although it would not be until much later that the phrase came into being. In 1908, Jack London's novel *The Iron Heel* contained a chapter called "Slaves of the Machine" in which his socialist hero, Ernest Everhard, declares that "no one today is a free agent. We are all caught in the wheels and cogs of the industrial machine." Note that it was not just the workers who had become slaves, it was everyone, from the mechanic to the mandarins and industrialists at the top of the heap: "Look at the reporters . . . and the editors that run the papers," Everhard declaims. "You will find them all slaves of the machine."[9]

The mark of a slave is obligatory submission to a higher authority. In the case of technology, since so many levels of modern society are dependent on machines, that higher authority must be the machine itself, the personified version of technology to which George Bush turned when confronted with the reality of Hurricane Katrina. We are all slaves, and technology is our master.

This is what Ursula Franklin meant when she noted that, while it is true that technology has bestowed many benefits on humanity (and, in any case, we cannot disinvent the wheel), it has also created "a culture of compliance"[10] in which we meekly submit to the dictates of the machine. Our compliance and conformity to technology — seen in our collective belief that every new technological device is an advance, that progress is synonymous with continuous technological innovation, and that as we become more technologically sophisticated we also become more civilized — not only ensures the continued use of technology, but weakens any resistance to what she calls "the programming of people." We don't seem to care that our cellular phones are tiny global-positioning devices by which our movements can be tracked by anyone with the right technology; that information from our credit-card purchases is used to tailor the ads we receive on our televisions and our computers; or that banks are more likely to give us loans if we have poor credit ratings than if we have no credit rating at all. We don't care because we are happy to have cell phones, credit cards and bank loans: we don't care because we have been programmed to see these infringements of civil liberty either as benefits or as the price of progress.

"Programmed" is a verb borrowed from computer technology. It is a measure of the degree to which we have been programmed that we believe the human brain can be conditioned like a machine. A recent book about computers, for example, contains the phrase: "Thinking takes energy, of course, but it needn't take much. The ultimate 'computer,' our own brain, uses only ten watts of power."[11] The technological mindset has never been so clearly expressed, unless it is in a recent ExxonMobil ad that shows a series of interconnected gears, and below each gear is a smiling human being, with the text: "Many parts working together — the only way to solve the world's energy challenges."

The problem with such statements is that they appear to be logical, even true. Many parts working together, as in a well-oiled machine, does seem like a good thing. But imitating a machine is not the *only* way to solve the world's energy challenges. First of all, we don't have an energy challenge, we have a serious energy crisis. And it is arguably well-oiled machines that have caused the crisis. Another way to "solve" the "challenge" might be to stop thinking like parts of a machine and to start thinking for ourselves.

There are two areas in which a closer look at our relationship with machines reveals the dangers associated with relying on technology to "solve" our "challenges." One is the tendency of a potentially beneficial avenue of technological research to veer off into the trivial. The other is the deadly connection between technology and war.

Technological innovations often tend toward the frivolous. In 1735, French inventor Jacques de Vaucanson constructed a mechanical duck that waddled, quacked, flapped its wings, splashed around in a tank of water, drank, ate, digested and excreted pellets of artificial food. The "automaton" was the size of a living duck and contained more than 1,000 moving parts. One wing alone was made of more than 400 separate mechanisms. Inside the duck was a rubber tube that functioned as a digester; it was the first-known use of rubber. So much mechanical genius, so much cutting-edge technology to make a toy.

Throughout the ages, people of inventive genius have racked their brains to come up with what modern physicist Freeman Dyson calls "toys for the rich."[12] For example, the first steam engine, the precursor of the machine that would one day change the course of Western history, was Hero of Alexandria's *aeolipile*, or wind wheel, a copper sphere containing water suspended over a fire. When the water boiled, steam escaped through two elbowed tubes that caused the sphere to spin on its axis. Period. Hero, who lived from AD 10 to AD 70, was one of the foremost scientists of his day, and yet is known chiefly for designing this curious but essentially useless gadget as well as a mechanical puppet theater operated by strings turned on a cylindrical cogwheel. It's as though 2,000 years from now Thomas Edison were known only as the inventor of the electric toothbrush.

The best that can be said for such devices is that they provide amusement, and there is some social value in being amused. Vaucanson made a fortune displaying his automaton, and had many imitators. But he is remembered today, if at all, as the builder of the mechanical duck rather than as the inventor of the geared apparatus that turned spindles on a silk loom, a device of far more social significance.

Another way to look at gadgets is that they turn potential socially beneficial advances into moneymaking spin-offs. As Chris Hedges notes in *Empire of Illusion*, technological side-shows create an illusion of prosperity and contentment that is actually intended to divert our attention away from the fact that the country's political and economic elite have "destroyed our manufacturing sector, looted the treasury, corrupted our democracy, and trashed the financial system." By luring us into continuing to believe that "the tickets to success, prosperity and happiness were waiting around the corner,"[13] technological gadgets create a culture of complacency as well as of compliance.

The trivialization of potentially powerful tools for social interaction into forms of amusement, or sources of profit, diminishes us as human beings. Rather than being enlightened and ennobled by the tremendous opportunities technology gives us to communicate and to educate — to connect with other people, with our environment and with ourselves — we are diverted by distractions and entertainments. For example, I've heard people complain that a certain organization's website is "too boring to bother with." This attitude threatens to trivialize the Internet by forcing it from a tremendous tool for education and information exchange into a vehicle for entertainment. That is precisely what happened with television. In 1927, Aldous Huxley, author of the novel *Brave New World*, wrote that "thanks to machinery, the common man enjoys today an amount of leisure undreamed of by his predecessors," which he saw as a good thing because leisure and prosperity make possible the acquisition of culture. Unfortunately, he added, "a great many men and women do not want to be cultured." He was writing too early for television, which, invented in 1926, had yet to disappoint. But he lamented that "the press, the cinema, the radio, the phonograph are not used . . . to propagate culture, but its opposite." The standardization of products fostered by mass production and the assembly line, he believed, had led to "the standardization of ideas."[14] Whereas culture, like nature, thrives on diversity.

This default into triviality has blighted one of the most potentially beneficial advances in modern medicine: nanotechnology. First proposed in 1989 by nuclear physicist Richard Feynman, nanotechnology is the manufacture of tiny mechanical robots so microscopically small that thousands of them, pre-programmed to seek out and kill cancer cells, for example, or repair tissue damaged by Parkinson's disease, or deliver drugs to infected areas, can be injected into the bloodstream. It is what has been called a "general-purpose technology," like rail travel, electricity or the Internet, with equally broad potential for revolutionizing society. After years of intense research and development, however, nanotechnologists have been able to come up with only the easy stuff: pants that won't stain, floor tiles that won't chip and self-cleaning windows. As with many cutting-edge technologies, the huge benefits are always just around the corner.

Carl von Clausewitz's book *On War*, published in 1812, remains the most influential treatise on military strategy ever written and is still taught in military academies around the world. It is the work that defined "war" as "the continuation of state policy by other means." Clausewitz identified three principle elements of war — he called them the "remarkable trinity" — that any army requires for victory: primordial violence, hatred and enmity; the recognition of the roles of chance and probability; and subordination to a rational policy. In the 200 years and many wars that have passed since Clausewitz's death in 1831, only one element has been added to his list by modern strategists: superior technology. "War," writes contemporary military historian Martin L. van Creveld, "is permeated by technology, and governed by it."[15]

We have been conditioned to accept technology, and with technology and war so closely allied, we have been conditioned to accept war. A list of the tools and machines that were developed for military purposes comprises many of the major inventions in human history. The stirrup, for example. The earliest known use of stirrups was in western China during the Jin Dynasty (300 BC). Before that, single stirrups were used to make it easier (and faster) for a rider to mount a horse: with two stirrups, the rider could control a horse while keeping both hands free to operate a weapon. It was Gothic horsemen using high-backed, or cantled, saddles and stirrups who defeated the formidable but stirrupless Roman cavalry at Adrianople in the fourth century AD, thus presaging the fall of the Roman Empire. Then, as now, battles were won by the army with superior technology.

After the fall of Rome, the armored horse archer and lancer evolved into the medieval knight-in-armor, familiar from Arthurian legends, who then dominated the battlefield. By the twelfth century, the knight's helm completely enclosed the head, and chain mail protected the hands and feet. Complete body armor did not come into use until the late fourteenth century, and although it was evidence of highly skilled metal workers, blacksmiths and armorers, it was often so heavy that knights wearing it could barely move, and served as little more than human battering rams.

The growing complexity and weight of the knight's armor — and therefore the growing uselessness of the knight — was a direct result of the ever-increasing destructiveness of the technology used against it. By the mid-thirteenth century, the mighty Welsh longbow was strong enough to pierce light chain mail. The later crossbows, which were hand-held, mechanized adaptations of Roman siege weapons, could fire short, steel-headed arrows, called "quarrels," through metal armor from a distance of 400 meters (437 yards). But even these formidable weapons were rendered out of date by the introduction, in the late thirteenth century, of another Chinese invention: gunpowder.

Black powder was invented in China in the tenth century. At first it was used exclusively for fireworks, but at the time fireworks were exclusively military: they were lit to send signals from a fleet's flagship, or between battalions in battle. Within 200 years, however, gunpowder's inherent destructiveness was being exploited. A mural in the Ta-tsu Cave in Szechuan Province, dating from AD 1128, shows two figures, one holding a round object with smoke pouring out of it, evidently a kind of grenade, and the other brandishing a long, tubular apparatus with a blast of fire emanating from its open end — the world's first depiction of a gun. Soon Arabian fusiliers were holding bamboo guns reinforced with steel bands packed with gunpowder and shooting arrows.

A hundred years later, gunpowder had been introduced to Europe. In 1266 the English natural scientist Roger Bacon described it, in *The Mirror of Alchemy*, as "a greater horror then those that come by Nature." He was not talking about fireworks: "A little matter fitted to the quantitie of a thumbe," he wrote, "maketh a horrible noise, and wonderfull lightning . . . whereby any citie and armie may be destroyed."[16] A later English document, *On the Majesty, Wisdom and Prudence of Kings*, by Walter de Milamete, dated 1327, contains the first European drawing of a cannon. As historian J.D. Bernal noted, "gunpowder and the cannon not only blew up the medieval world economically and politically; they were the major forces in destroying its system of ideas."[17] Gunpowder greatly enhanced our ability to kill at a distance, further distancing us from the reality of our actions, and increasing our alienation from nature.

More examples of the connection between technology and war abound. The first airplane the Wright brothers sold was to the US Army Signal Corps for use during the First World War. At first, biplanes were used for reconnaissance, but soon airborne soldiers were dropping bombs into enemy trenches. Similarly, the jet engine was not developed for commercial airlines; it was first fitted into fighter aircraft during the Second World War. And atomic energy was originally harnessed not for peaceful purposes, such as heating buildings or producing electricity, but to create two atomic bombs that killed hundreds of thousands of Japanese civilians in 1945. Super glue was first developed in 1942 for making clear plastic gunsights. Radar, which has been called "the invention that changed the world" for its links to everything from airport and weather tracking systems to TV and computer screens to microwave ovens, was perfected in the 1940s at the Massachusetts Institute of Technology (MIT) for the detection of incoming enemy aircraft during the Second World War. Even the Internet was first conceived by the US Defense Department in 1963, during the Cold War. It was intended to link a group of military computers so that in the event of a nuclear attack, users could communicate with one another, wherever they were located.

For Lewis Mumford, the link between machines and war altered his view of technology. In *The Myth of the Machine: Technics and Civilization* (1934), he referred to large collections of human workers as "megamachines," which he defined as conglomerations of rigid, hierarchical social organization along the lines of ant colonies. Originally he viewed megamachines as positives: it was the Egyptian megamachine, for example, that built the pyramids. Thousands of human beings, each functioning as single parts in a huge machine (as in the ExxonMobil ad mentioned previously), accomplished far more than the same number of people working independently or in small groups, and the pyramids fulfilled a valuable social function, since they were, in effect, temples.

By 1970, however, Mumford's tune had changed. He was no longer enthusiastic about the power wielded by the megamachine. In *The Myth of the Machine: The Pentagon of Power*, he writes that "the megamachine has become a negative entity." What had happened between 1934 and 1970 to change Mumford's mind about technological society? The Second World War and its aftermath. To Mumford's horror, he saw Nazi Germany as a vast, efficient megamachine, the goal of which was genocide and world domination. The Soviet Union, founded on secrecy and suppression, was another. And the United States, "the modernized megamachine," he noted, emerged between 1940 and 1961 with the transformation of the American military, industrial and scientific establishments into a single, concentrated complex that produced, among other things, the atom bomb.[18] More recently it has produced Guantanamo Bay, which novelist J.M. Coetzee has described as "a machine for inflicting pain and humiliation on the other."[19]

The American Declaration of Independence, signed in 1776, guaranteed each of its (white, male, adult) citizens the right to "life, liberty, and the pursuit of happiness." Since then, the definitions of those rights have changed. Machines are now able to tell us exactly when life begins and ends, and happiness has become associated with the acquisition of more and more sophisticated machines. If we are truly slaves of the machine, then the traditional concept of liberty must be adjusted as well.

But recent studies show that, once our basic material needs are met, what really makes us happy today are the same things that made human beings happy at the dawn of civilization. In a study of happiness in many countries and cultures, including developed and developing countries, social scientist Carol Graham found that most people, when asked what made them happy, mentioned such simple pleasures as good health, the proximity of friends and family members, and access to education. None of these things necessarily requires technology. In countries where these basic needs are met, few talk about money, success, power or the accumulation of material goods.

"And yet," she says, "the pursuit of material goods still dominates our idea of what makes us happy, often at the expense of the simpler things that really do make us happy."[20] No one, for example, placed owning an MP3 player above earning the respect of others on their scale of what made them happy, but it is possible that many felt that owning an MP3 player was what earned them the respect of others. Put another way, there is a persistent belief that the more stuff we have, the happier we will be — a belief that shows how thoroughly we have been programmed by technology — but the fact that we still define happiness in simpler terms indicates how shallow that programming really is. It is untrue, for example, that we become happier as we become richer, or that we enjoy more leisure time today than we did fifty years ago. In fact, on average, North Americans worked three more hours a week in 2000 than they did in 1960, probably because our annual consumption had risen from $12,000 to $24,000 in that time, and we had to work longer hours to pay for it. And still we weren't "happy." Studies of lottery winners show that as our material wealth increases, so do our expectations of further material wealth, keeping us in a constant state of unhappiness. The more stuff we have, the more stuff we want. We become stuck on the "hedonic treadmill," or the state in which our expectations rise at the same pace as our incomes, and the happiness we expect from our lifestyles remains constantly out of reach.

At what point in human history did we start to behave as though material wealth and the acquisition of goods would lead to happiness, when clearly we do not truly believe that to be the case? Another way to phrase the question is, when did we become a domesticated species and appoint technology as our master? How did we get on this "hedonic treadmill"? And how can we step off it?

Chapter 2
Technology and the Control of Nature

In 1991, hikers in the Italian Alps made a gruesome discovery. Frozen into the Schnalstal Glacier, beginning to emerge as the ice melted, was the body of a man, perfectly preserved but, to judge by his clothes, from another century. Indeed, when the body was removed and examined by scientists, it turned out to have been encased in glacial ice for the past 5,300 years. Ötzi the Iceman, as he came to be called, was nearly as old as human civilization itself.

Ötzi's clothes and the contents of his pouch tell us a lot about the state of technology at his time. He was wearing a hat, a coat and leggings manufactured from a variety of animal skins, cut into strips and sewn together with leather string. His bear-hide shoes were lined with grass, for warmth, and seemed to have been at one time attached to snowshoes. He carried a yew longbow and, slung over his shoulder, a quiver containing fourteen arrows with stone points and feather flight stabilizers. He wore a belt with a sheath holding a flint knife with an ash handle; he also had a copper ax with a yew handle. In a pouch, there were pieces of flint and pyrite for starting fires, a scraper, a drill, a bone awl, a bit of antler, and birch-bark baskets containing berries and two species of mushrooms.

It was a very basic, practical tool kit: Ötzi carried everything he needed for his immediate survival, and nothing else. He was obviously no stranger to technology, but the tools he had were simple. He could kill game, cut wood for cooking and heating, prepare skins, sew his own clothing, and even make his own arrowheads. But his acquaintance with technology did not change his relationship with his environment in any fundamental way. They simply made survival easier.

Ursula Franklin distinguishes between two kinds of technology: work-related and control-related technologies. The former refers to the kinds of tools and techniques that Ötzi knew: basic tools that make work easier for the worker. A shovel is a piece of work-related technology. So is a computer. Both exist simply to make a job easier to perform. A shovel makes it easier to dig a hole than if the worker had to use his or her bare hands; a computer, by itself, simply facilitates the task of data storage and retrieval, a task that has been performed by hand by librarians and archivists since ancient times. Computers can do complicated calculations and make complex connections faster than humans can, but they are only as skilled as the humans who program them.

Human beings expend less energy when using work-related technologies, and although a worker can complete a task faster with work-related technology, speed is not an end in itself. Working more quickly and producing more goods may be a by-product of work-related technology, but it is not its goal. With work-related technologies, a single worker is able to complete all the aspects of a project from start to finish. Having the proper tools, a single worker can make a chair, performing all the various tasks a chair involves, from cutting down a tree to obtain wood, to whittling or lathing the legs and rungs, to growing and twisting the hemp with which to weave the seat.

Work-related technology often results in the worker doing a better job. A carpenter can make a better table using saws, planes and screwdrivers than he or she can without them. This results in benefits to society and the individual worker: society gets a better-made, better-looking and longer-lasting table, and the carpenter feels pride in his or her accomplishment, and gains the respect of his or her peers. In the past, workers using work-related technologies identified so closely with their work that they often took their employment as their surname: Carpenter, Tailor, Weaver, Fletcher, Mason. It is highly unlikely that, in the future, there will be people with surnames like Production Manager, Data Processor or Assembly-Line Worker (although the name Webster may take on new significance).

If we attach a meter to a shovel and allow a supervisor to monitor the amount of dirt a worker lifts with it in a day, we turn work-related technology into control-related technology. Franklin defines control-related technologies as "those developments that do not primarily address the process of work with the aim of making it easier, but try to increase control over the operation."[1] She gives the example of word processors. One word processor is work-related; it is little more than a glorified typewriter. But when ten word processors are linked together to a central computer, they become control-related devices, since in such a linked system, the performance of each worker can be monitored by an overseer and the quantity of their work recorded and assessed. A worker's performance can be assessed, but only by criteria that can be measured by a machine — by speed and efficiency. In other words, by quantitative rather than qualitative analyses.

The assembly line, put into operation by Henry Ford in 1913 but based on the division-of-labor principle instituted during the Industrial Revolution, is another example of control-related technology. Each worker is responsible for completing a single, small step in the overall assembly of the product. Instead of one multiskilled craftsperson completing an entire chair, a dozen unskilled laborers divide up the tasks, so that one of them saws the wood, another turns the rungs on a lathe, another the legs, and so on. A chair can be made more quickly and more efficiently this way. At the Ford plant in Dearborn, Michigan, in the 1920s, workers assembled Model Ts so quickly that a new car rolled off the assembly line every three minutes, but few of those workers were able to take pride in their work. The entire Ford plant functioned like a machine, with each worker in it a small, anonymous, replaceable part. Ford revolutionized the way manufacturing was carried out in the United States, and the Model T made transportation available to vast numbers of people, but mass production favors quantity over quality, and job satisfaction all but disappears.

Ötzi was probably not a simple hunter-gatherer. Examination of his possessions showed that his shoes were made by a skilled cobbler, his copper ax had been hammered by a metal worker, and his arrows appear to have been made by a fletcher. Ötzi belonged to a people who had migrated north from present-day Greece and Macedonia in 6200 BC, settled around the Black Sea and spread into the Lower Danube Valley. They lived in large towns containing as many as 2,000 houses. Basically an agrarian culture, they had brought with them wheat and barley seeds, domesticated cattle and sheep. They had ceramics and, around 5400 BC, developed copper smelting. They used both to produce work-related technology such as cooking pots, and well-crafted objects of religious and decorative art, including statuettes of iconic figures and jewelry. They did not confuse art with entertainment, as our own culture does. Art draws us into thinking more deeply about the world around us; entertainment diverts us from thinking deeply about anything. Although they had no written language, the people of Old Europe belonged to a highly sophisticated culture.

It may have been their Greek origins. Agriculture,

developed in the Middle East shortly after the retreat of the last Ice Age, first spread into the Mediterranean countries, including Egypt, Greece and Italy, before fanning out into Asia and the rest of Europe. Based solely on work-related technology, agriculture encouraged individuals to live and work together in groups, which required skills in communication and organization that eventually, around 2600 BC, led to Mumford's "megamachine" culture that built the pyramids in Egypt.[2]

But Greece did not develop into a megamachine. When the spirit of scientific enquiry arose in ancient Greece around 1500 BC, it was a purely intellectual activity, deliberately kept separate from practical application. The Greeks placed small value on the needs of the body, preferring the life of the mind. They valued the abstract above the utilitarian: they developed mathematics, philosophy, music, poetry, drama and politics, not as spurs to action, but as lures to contemplation.

To be sure, the Greeks made many important technological advances. The city of Athens enjoyed a sophisticated system of water delivery and sewage disposal. The Greeks knew about hydraulics: the Alexandrian inventor Ctesibius was known as "the father of pneumatics" for his work with compressed air. By the fourteenth century BC, Greek engineers had drained Lake Kopaida, the largest lake in Greece, by drilling a 2.23-kilometer (1.38-mile) tunnel through solid rock between the lake and the Aegean Sea. The Greeks had windmills, catapults, cranes, compound pulleys, gears and the lever. But, like Hero of Alexandria, they did not count these achievements among their major contributions to Western civilization. Mechanical devices were simply illustrations of philosophical or mathematical principles, not buffers between themselves and their environment, or a means of controlling the population. Hero of Alexandria's whirling steam engine was not employed to lift heavy weights or turn cranks — that didn't happen for another 1,700 years. As far as the Greeks were concerned, lifting heavy objects was work for slaves. Once a mathematical theorem was demonstrated, there was no further need for the apparatus that provided the proof. The Greeks did not think as a technological society.

The Romans, on the other hand, specialized in control-based technology. It is interesting that, unlike the Greeks, the Romans took their name not from the land, but from the city they built at the heart of it: Rome, the first megacity. At its height in the first century BC, the Roman Empire had a population of about 60 million people, of whom only 1 million or 2 million lived in Rome (accounts vary), and yet the entire extended territory took its definition from the central authoritative body. It was as though everyone in the United States were to call themselves Washingtonians. Rome was all about control, and control was maintained largely through the application of technology.

Rather than keep science and technology separate, the Romans combined the two, and seemed interested only in science that led directly to some practical, control-oriented implementation. Much of what the Romans knew of science they received from elsewhere, in some cases literally, since after the fall of Greece to Rome in the first century BC, many Greek scholars became slaves and tutors in aristocratic Roman households.[3] Technology found in Pompeii, the Roman city preserved by ash falling from the eruption of Mount Vesuvius — the mill wheel (turned by human or animal power), the treadmill crane (operated by two people walking inside a huge wooden wheel), the dual-action suction pump — were Greek inventions. In architecture, the much-celebrated Roman arch was copied from the Etruscans. Most of the tools in a Roman carpenter's toolbox — the try square, the plumb line, the chalk line, the A-level — had been known in ancient Egypt, which had become part of the Roman Empire and supplied Rome with most of its wheat and a lot of its science. Roman culture was imperialist, that is to say acquisitive, rather than inventive. When the Romans needed something, they took it.

To build the pyramids, the Egyptians had applied social organization to a technological problem. The Romans did the opposite: they applied technical thinking to social organization. At the time of Julius Caesar, who died in 44 BC, Rome was divided into hundreds of internal divisions, or *insulae*, each containing a *myriad*, or 10,000, people. Each division had its own internal social and political organization, what today would be called an "infrastructure," and it is in this technical arena of city planning — architecture, road construction, food delivery, water in and sewage out, medicine, governance and jurisprudence — that the Romans excelled. Rome worked as a city because of the organizational genius of its administrators. The city, and eventually the whole Roman Empire under Caesar's successor, Octavian, functioned as one colossal machine.

Feeding the juggernaut demanded a dedicated and technologically savvy farming class as well as engineers to build the efficient networks of roads and aqueducts needed to deliver food and water to the city. Roads were built by the military and remained a military responsibility: they were ordered by consuls and senators, designed by army surveyors, and built by soldiers. At its peak, the Roman road network totaled more than 85,000 kilometers (52,800 miles) and stretched over modern-day Italy, Britain, France, Germany, Poland and Egypt. The road system was more than a way of making it easier to get food into the city; it was a way of controlling the far-flung borders of the empire. Roman legions could cover a lot of distance on those arrow-straight, paved and drained roadways. Consuls in Rome could keep in steady touch with the outlying districts and learn quickly of any trouble or insurrection. The roads were a control-based technology. Roads were to the Romans what the Internet is to our era: a widespread, well-maintained public communications system.

In other areas, the Romans proved equally practical and systematic. Roman engineers dammed rivers and made huge cement-lined reservoirs to supply a vast network of aqueducts that carried water for hundreds of miles to towns and the city. Roman farmers pioneered the practice of breeding and training animals for labor. Romans improved on the hand-held sickle by curving the metal blade and attaching a wooden handle at an angle, and they invented the scythe. Roman farmers understood manure. In Gaul, they invented a mechanical harvester that, when pulled by a team of oxen, cut the heads off the wheat, leaving the stalks still rooted in the ground (later to be cut for straw) and collected the grain in a trailing basket. Early mill wheels were turned by slaves or by donkeys, but in 20 BC they invented the water mill.

In order to keep its city-bound citizens fed, Rome traded with lands as far away as Africa and Asia, augmenting its own list of crops with exotics from the Caucasus (quince), northern Eurasia (apples), Central Asia (millet and cumin), India (cucumber, sesame, citrus fruits) and China (chicken, rice, apricots, peaches). The need for food, and the consequent demand for technology to import, transport and adapt new species to growing conditions on the Italian peninsula, committed the Romans to maintaining and defending a trade network so vast and complex that the effort eventually contributed to the defeat of the empire.

Control-oriented technological systems tend to collapse under their own weight. They are, literally, against nature, since nature (including human nature) is the element such systems are designed to control. Quite often they contain within them the seeds of their own collapse. For example, people caught up in a control-oriented technology often retain an inner yearning for a less regimented way of living, as in the opening lines of Wilkie Collins' novel *The Woman in White*, published in 1860 in the aftermath of the Industrial Revolution: "The weary pilgrims of the London pavements were beginning to think of the cloud-shadows on the corn-fields and the autumn breezes on the sea-shore."[4] Such people eventually rebel against the regimentation of the technological mindset. It is interesting that when fundamentalist Islamic groups wanted to attack what they saw as the US imperialist machine — symbolized by the twin towers of New York's World Trade Center — on September 11, 2001, they chose airplanes as their weapons, specifically airplanes that had been designed and built in the US and belonged to US-owned airlines.

The beginning of the decline of the Roman Empire has been linked to its acceptance of Christianity. Whether the adoption of Christianity's simplified social credo weakened the hierarchy's grasp of its citizens' minds, or the rise of Christianity coincided with an already existing dissatisfaction with Roman rigidity, the Roman Empire began to fall about the time the Roman emperor Constantine converted to Christianity in AD 313.

But as Lewis Mumford observes, often when a new idea becomes incorporated into an existing institution, it "loses some of its original purity, if it does not in fact turn into its own antithesis through the very act of materialization."[5] In other words, when an abstract concept like "freedom" becomes part of a regime based on intolerance, the ideal of freedom becomes diluted. For example, the emancipation of slaves in the US in 1865, following the Civil War, did not actually give former slaves the "freedom" they had been hoping for. A more recent example took place in the 1980s, when the Soviet Union relaxed its exclusion of Western influences and admitted a degree of capitalism into its social structure. The result was a corrupt form of capitalism, a black-market mercantilism that presaged, if it did not bring about, the collapse of the Soviet system. In Roman times, when the state converted to Christianity, the Christian Church also took on some of the aspects of the Roman state. From a simple, desert religion advocating monotheism and tolerance, it became an organized urban institution as complex and hierarchical as the Roman state. In short, it became the Roman Catholic Church, a megamachine fully as powerful and control-oriented as the Roman Empire that preceded it.

The Catholic Church controlled Europe for the next eleven centuries. Through the hierarchy of the Church, which mirrored that of imperial Rome — the Pope as Caesar, bishops and priests divided into Secretariats, Congregations, Tribunals, Pontifical Councils, and various Offices — the Church governed every aspect of its adherents' lives. The institution had its own laws, owned vast properties and even imposed its own taxes in the form of tithes. Catholics were told when to pray, what language to pray in, what to read, what to eat, even when and how to have sex.

At first, Church leaders were wary of technological advances. Anything that came from the human mind, they held, rather than from the word of God, was viewed with suspicion and intolerance. Science, art and philosophy, if they were to exist at all, had to further the glory of God (i.e., the power of the Church), not the convenience of humankind. It was God, not humans, who made things, and it was through faith, not knowledge, that we approached perfection.

By the fourth century, however, some religious thinkers began to question the split between the works of humans and the workings of God. Perhaps, they said, it was God who put the idea for new machines into the minds of their human makers. If God caused humans to create a thing, the fourth-century philosopher Gregory of Nyssa asked, then who were we to say that it was without merit? If God didn't want us to till the land, then why did he allow us to invent the plow?

The argument was powerful enough to make Church leaders gradually give in to it, bringing about an actual merger between technology and religion. By inventing new machines, humans were actually extending and completing God's work. In the Bible, the Garden of Eden was a planted garden; by breaking new land and planting new crops, humans were recreating God's original Paradise. And the more land that could be worked, the more rent and the greater the tithes that went to the

Church. Technology increased the wealth and the power of the clergy, and thus even work-related agricultural inventions like the heavy plow were indirectly power-related. A further point also became apparent to the Church fathers. Manual labor in the ancient world had mostly been supplied by slaves. While the Church in the early Middle Ages did not forbid slavery, especially of non-Christians, it did regard the ownership of slaves as sullying the spirit of Christianity. To the fourth-century Greek theologian St. John Chrysostom, for example, "slavery is the fruit of covetousness, of extravagance, of insatiable greediness."[6] The Church taught that all slaves and bondsmen should be treated humanely. Technological innovations reduced the amount of work to be done by humans and so reduced the need for slavery.

Eventually, religion and technology became easy bedfellows. As David Noble writes in *The Religion of Technology*, technology and religion "are merged, and always have been, the technological enterprise being, at the same time, an essentially religious endeavor."[7] Technology and religion strove for a similar goal: to improve the human condition and bring people closer to the ideal existence intended for them by God. Through technology, humans could recreate the conditions of the Garden of Eden. By means of technology, we sinners could be saved.

Technology also helped fulfill the Biblical injunction that humans must exercise dominion, or control, over animals. Animal husbandry — the domestication and use of wild animals such as goats, sheep and cattle — had been known for thousands of years. Oxen and horses had been used as beasts of burden in the classical world. The Romans invented harnesses that attached up to eight oxen to a single plow, so that fields could be worked more quickly and with less strain on each animal. But Roman harnesses were poorly designed, with the neck strap, or yoke, going around the animal's neck and the load affixed to straps that ran along the animal's back, pulling back its head and even choking it if the load were too heavy. This explains why farmers needed eight oxen to pull a light plow through the dry, thin Mediterranean soil, and why Roman law imposed a limit of 500 kilograms (1,100 pounds) on loads drawn by horse.

In northern countries, where the clay soils were heavier and less well drained, stronger and more efficient equipment was needed. In the sixth century, the neck strap was replaced by a breast strap, which fit across the animal's chest, with the load attached low on the sides so that the animal could pull using the strength of its shoulders and legs. Padded collars were introduced in the eighth century, and the whippletree — a bar that ran across the front of the wagon to distribute the load evenly among the animals — was added in the eleventh century.

These inventions gradually allowed horses to replace oxen. Horses were not as strong as oxen, but they worked faster: work that took three days with oxen could be done in two days with horses. And to the technological mindset, faster is always better. Workhorses also allowed farmers to produce more crops, which was important not only to the Church but to the general populace, since the greatest limiting factor in European population growth during the Middle Ages was the shortage of food, particularly grain.

From the tenth to the thirteenth centuries, as the European population exploded (from approximately 25 million in AD 400 to nearly 100 million by 1300), people moved out of concentrated semi-urban areas into hitherto uninhabited regions. They cut down forests and drained swamps, and with their improved farming implements cleared more land, grew more wheat and fed more people. At the same time, cities expanded. As the old walled cities increased in population, secondary walls were constructed outside the original walls, and in Europe most of these secondary walls date from the tenth century. Serfs left the land and moved into the cities, where they were called "villeins." Cities became places of industry rather than simple commercial centers, and technological changes kept pace with developments in the areas represented by the four "m's": manufacture, mining, metallurgy and milling. With an ever-expanding work force, advances in these areas gradually took the form of control-related technologies, in order that work proceed not only more rapidly, but more efficiently and therefore more profitably.

For example, the rise of cities created a merchant class, and merchants required a transportation system more extensive than that provided by the old Roman network of roads. This led to the improvement of sailing vessels. Roman ships had had fore-and-aft sails, later called lateens, or latin-rigged, triangular sails, attached to long booms that ran from the bow and crossed the main-mast. Viking vessels were square sailed, which allowed swift movement through the water — when the wind was favorable. When it wasn't, square-rigged and larger lateen-rigged ships had to be propelled by oarsmen, who were almost always slaves. And they could not tack or sail close to the wind.

By the fourteenth century, multiple lateen sails were rigged on larger, broad-beamed vessels that could be sailed without oarsmen. As well, fixed, swinging rudders attached to the ships' sterns meant that the ships could be navigated almost directly into the wind rather than having to wait until the wind was more obliging. Such inventions greatly expanded the areas from which raw materials could be gathered for manufacture, as well as the countries in which the finished products could be marketed.

Windmills were in general use in China in the seventh century and were introduced into Europe during the twelfth. Water mills also gained importance during the Middle Ages. The Romans had used them to drive saws with which to cut marble for building; in the fourteenth century they were adapted to drive fulling mills for cleaning and thickening wool cloth, as well as to oper-ate bellows and forge-hammers in blacksmithing shops. Water-driven pumps were used to pump water out of the deeper mine shafts now required to furnish metalworkers with raw materials.

Many technological items that we think of as belonging to modern times are actually medieval in origin. The mechanical clock, for instance, which is now symbolic of technology-related pressure, is said to have been invented by a French monk, Gerbert d'Aurillac, who in AD 999 became Pope Sylvester II. Whether or not Gerbert was its genius, the mechanical clock was quickly adopted by Benedictine monks, for whom it regulated bell ringing in the striking of the seven canonical hours decreed in the seventh century by Pope Sabinianus to regulate monastic life. Until then, these hours had been determined by guesswork, by ancient water clocks that worked on the dubious notion that water dripped out of a vessel at a steady rate, by sundials that obviously didn't work at night and less obviously varied according to latitude, or even by notched candles.

Organic time, the timing dictated by nature, is far from exact. Farmers may define spring as the time when their ewes lamb, or recognize autumn as the season when their crops are harvested, but such measurements fluctuate from year to year, country to country, and even from farm to farm. Before the mechanical clock, the ringing of canonical hours varied with the seasons (winter could freeze the water in a water clock), the weather (clouds could render the sundial useless) and the whims of monks in different abbeys. Organic time offends the technological mind as much as organic food does. It represents nature running out of control. With mechanical clocks, sext could be rung at twelve o'clock sharp, whether it was summer or winter, France or Germany, cloudy or clear. Mechanical clocks put nature on a leash.

By the thirteenth century, there were 40,000 Benedictine monasteries in Europe, each of them ordered in military precision by mechanical clocks. Soon, most large towns had clock towers, and city life was as regulated as life in a monastery. Canonical hours became the hours of the workday: stores and offices opened at nine (terce), lunch was at noon (sext), and people went home at sunset (vespers). Shop clerks and industry workers were paid by the hour, not by the piece. People were valued for their punctuality, industries for their efficiency — the number of articles they could produce in an hour, or a day — rather than by the quality of their work or their wares. Lewis Mumford sees in Benedictine medieval monasteries the impetus that "helped give human enterprise the regular, collective beat and rhythm of the machine; for the clock is not merely a means of keeping track of the hours, but of synchronizing the actions of men."[8]

By the middle of the fourteenth century, the hours a clock measured were divided into sixty minutes, and the minute into sixty seconds. Today we are accustomed to time expressed in thousandths of a second. Whether an Olympic athlete wins or loses, for instance, is a question that can only be determined by machines. Time is divided into entirely arbitrary divisions, useful only if everyone on Earth agrees to them. Time becomes an abstract product of the human mind rather than a concrete aspect of organic nature. With the mechanical clock, humans moved closer to living in an environment constructed by themselves — the whole world, in a sense, has become a Benedictine monastery. In so doing, we moved away from what makes us truly happy, for as Leo Tolstoy observed, "one of the conditions of happiness is that the link between Man and Nature shall not be broken." Technology exists to break that link.

Chapter 3
The Renaissance

"Renaissance" means "rebirth" and refers to the period, beginning in the first half of the fifteenth century and extending into the early seventeenth, when the pure sciences and arts of the classical Greek period were rediscovered, or reborn, in Europe. The impetus for this leap out of the Dark Ages was the discovery and translation of classical treatises that had been destroyed or (as Umberto Eco suggests in his novel *The Name of the Rose*) hidden away by the Church. Many of the texts had continued to exist in Arabic translations, and news of these books was probably brought to Europe by returning Crusaders, by merchants trading in the Mongolian city of Tabriz or by missionaries who had been to the Far East. With the European adaptation of the Chinese invention of moveable type, many of these newly discovered texts were put into circulation, greatly broadening education and people's political understanding of the world. Renaissance Europe saw a burgeoning of activity in virtually all the scientific, intellectual and technological areas of everyday life.

Perhaps because of its link to classical Greece, the European Renaissance is often thought of as a brief artistic hiatus between the Middle Ages and the Industrial Revolution. Many of its principle participants were indeed artists: Shakespeare, Spenser and Marlowe in England, Boccaccio and Dante in Italy, Rabelais in France. Many of them embraced technology as a way of reaching the rapidly increasing audiences for their work. Architecture, for example, combined the art of drawing with the empirical science of building construction.

One of the Italian Renaissance's most eminent architects was Leon Battista Alberti, who wrote that an architect was one "who, by sure and wonderful art and method, is able both with thought and invention to devise and with execution to complete all those works which, by means of the movement of great weights, and the conjunction and amassment of bodies, can with the greatest beauty be adapted to the uses of mankind."[1]

The Italian painter, sculptor and mathematician Filippo Brunelleschi (1377-1446), who invented linear perspective in painting, also designed and oversaw the building of the vaulted dome of the Basilica di Santa Maria del Fiore in Florence, still the largest brick dome ever constructed.

By promoting the social benefits of technology, thereby making technological innovation acceptable to an artistic sensibility, the Renaissance contained the seeds of the Industrial Revolution. It was during this period that small cottage-based industries started to be turned into factories. In 1540, the Italian metallurgist Vannoccio Biringuccio published *De la pirotechnia* (*Work in Fire*), the first comprehensive textbook on metallurgy, in which he describes methods for smelting gold, silver, copper, lead, tin and iron that had formerly been the secret knowledge of guildsmen. As a result, metal foundries sprang up across Europe. Biringuccio's book was followed in 1556 by *De re metallica* (*On Metallurgy*), by Georgius Agricola. Such works both reflected and fostered the expansion of the use of metals, mostly for domestic purposes such as jewelry and decorative household items, but also for producing goods for trade in an expanding international market. England, for example, although its principle export during the Renaissance period was woolen goods, also traded large quantities of tin and pewter, and imported in return raw iron from Spain as well as haberdashery items such as pins, buttons, buckles, brooches and houseware from around Europe. Even at this early stage of mercantilism, massive machinery was put in place for the purpose of mass producing trinkets.

Both Biringuccio and Agricola provided instructions and illustrations of inventions for improving mining methods in order to increase output and to supply the growing demand for metallurgy products. Mines were dug deeper, as a result, and when they filled with water, mechanical means for pumping water out of them became vital. Also, Agricola describes horse-turned capstans (revolving cylinders used for winding ropes and cables) and huge water wheels that moved bellows for pumping air down the mines, and drive shafts for lifting ore from their depths. When surface water to drive wheels wasn't available near the mines, rivers were diverted to them, or else elaborate systems of rods were constructed to transfer power from distant rivers to the mines, sometimes for a distance of several miles.

Renaissance mining and manufacturing continued the change in the relationship between Europeans and their environment that had begun in the Middle Ages. At the end of the Roman period, Europe was 80 percent covered by forest; by the end of the Renaissance, coverage was depleted to less than 20 percent. This became a serious problem as more and more industries requiring large amounts of fuel began to spring up. Shipbuilding and the growing requirements of urban populations consumed vast acreages of forest products: in England, the price of firewood increased during this period more rapidly than almost any other commodity. The new technologies required vast amounts of fuel. The extraction of salt from seawater by evaporation in great, heated pans, the manufacture of glass, bricks and tiles, the production of alum for the dyeing industry, and especially ironwork and copper smelting all required kilns and furnaces that burned enormous quantities of wood in the form of charcoal, especially after the introduction of the blast furnace to produce cast iron around 1540. Increasingly, wood had to be transported from the forests to the manufacturing area, which depleted forests, required extensive road building, sometimes over old Roman road beds, and also increased the costs of production.

The solution was to switch from using wood and charcoal as fuels to using black coal, a change that took place at the beginning of the sixteenth century. Coal had been known in China since about the fourth century and was mined in northern Europe from the twelfth century, but it was used mostly for home heating and was derived from shallow surface deposits that required little technology. During the sixteenth century, however, deep-shaft coal extraction in Holland and Belgium tripled and then quadrupled as the demand for smelters and blast furnaces soared.

It was in England, which had the most abundant near-surface coal seams in all of Europe, that coal mining rang the most significant changes for the future. Huge deposits were worked in areas such as Wollaton, on the Trent River, and Newcastle-upon-Tyne. In 1563, 33,000 tons of coal were shipped from Newcastle, mostly to London factories. By 1609, that figure had jumped to 252,000 tons and England was producing 2 million tons of coal a year. Coal turned the city of London into a manufacturing city and England into the industrial capital of the world — as well as the smog capital. In 1645, English writer John Evelyn compared London to "the picture of Troy sacked by the Greeks,"[2] as coal smoke rose from house chimneys and factory stacks and hung over the city in great, dark clouds.

Coal presaged the Industrial Age in several ways. Advances in the manufacture of iron were only possible with coal, which burned at higher temperatures than charcoal and therefore allowed the production of cast iron. Greater demand for coal prompted advances in mining technology, mostly in the area of removing water from ever deeper mine shafts: one out of every six patents granted in England during the reigns of Elizabeth I, James I and Charles I were related to pumping water. And the problem of moving coal from localities far from ports and navigable rivers also spurred the transportation industry. As early as 1598, coal carts in Wollaton were transported to boats on the Trent River by means of horse-drawn wagons pulled along wooden tracks called "tilting rails," precursors of the railway. It was these and other innovations made necessary by the adoption of coal that paved the way for the machine economy of the next three centuries.

It was during the Renaissance that designs for steam-driven engines began to circulate. Leonardo da Vinci designed one, although like many of Leonardo's ideas it was never built. Others did make it off the drawing board. In 1543, Blasco de Garay, a retired Spanish naval captain turned inventor, affixed a large copper boiler to two paddlewheels to move a 200-ton ship, *La Trinidad* (*Trinity*), a distance of two leagues in the port of Barcelona. Spanish authorities worried about the danger of the copper cauldron exploding, but de Garay had proven his point, and navigation had taken a giant leap.

Eyeglasses were used in China in the ninth century AD, but they were first introduced to Europe by glazers in Florence, Italy, in the late thirteenth. They were called "spectacles," a word coined by the Dominican friar Salcino de Armat in 1317. Chaucer refers to spectacles in "The Wife of Bath's Tale" around 1380, by which time they were common eyewear among clerks, scholars and clerics. The Italian Renaissance painter Dominico Ghirlandaio painted St. Jerome wearing a pair of eyeglasses in 1480, and from then on St. Jerome was the patron saint of the spectacle-makers' guild. The earliest lenses were ground not of glass but of clear crystal, usually a mineral known as beryl. In fifteenth-century Germany, spectacles were called *Berylle*, a word later contracted to *Brille*, the modern German word for eyeglasses. The English word "brilliant" is also derived from *Berylle*.

Although spectacles are a work-related technology — they make seeing easier — they had an enormous impact on society after the invention of the printing press, when reading became more widespread. Farsightedness is an affliction of old age, when seeing clearly at a distance is still possible, but it becomes more difficult to focus on an object held close to the face, like a book. Eyeglasses extended the useful life of the elderly, allowing them to participate longer in the greatly expanded opportunities for social interaction created by the proliferation of books. The elderly could not only read the work of others but could also write books themselves, ensuring that knowledge that might otherwise have been lost was passed on to future generations. The printing press was enormously instrumental in fomenting the great social and religious upheavals of the following centuries. But it might not have had such an impact had it not been for the invention of spectacles.

In the early Renaissance books were still being copied by hand on parchment, a slow and costly process that required the skins of twenty-five sheep for every 200-page book and could take up to ten years for a single volume. But by the early 1400s, printing houses using block type and manual rubbing or brushing were capable of running off multiple copies in a much shorter time. Still, the production of a book, even by a printer using the new rag paper, the technique of which had been acquired from the Islamic Empire in the twelfth century, was a long and arduous process.

Books were printed from woodblocks the size of one page, each block carved with the words and illustrations for that page alone: new page, new woodblock. Wood is a fragile material, the blocks would wear and split, and new blocks would need to be carved. Moveable type was an improvement. With each letter carved on a separate piece of wood or molded onto a ceramic tile, printers could produce entire books by rearranging individual letters to form a new page. Moveable type was developed by the Chinese in the eleventh century. In 1313, the Chinese printer Wang Zhen produced the *Nung Shu*, a treatise on agriculture, using moveable wooden type. The work contained 60,000 characters and had a print run of 100 copies.

Johannes Gutenberg didn't *invent* moveable type, then, but he perfected it. His innovations were a system of individual metal letters that lasted longer than wood or clay, and the adaptation of a letterpress based on the screw-type presses already used for pressing linen or crushing grapes and olives. Gutenberg's father was a Companion of the Mint in his hometown of Mainz, Germany, which was granted the right to circulate its own coinage in 1419. Coins were made by punching reversed letters and images into a flat disc of gold or silver; the punches were steel shafts, the tips of which were carved using extremely sharp graving tools.

Gutenberg made his type the same way, by carving letters backwards on a steel punch, then striking the shape of the letter into a copper block to form a mold. He then poured a compound of lead, tin and antimony into the mold to make his metal type. He originally made his molds in fine sand, but later switched to copper to achieve a permanent mold and sharper images. Gutenberg also invented an improved ink made of powdered charcoal ground in a linseed-oil varnish that worked better on metal type.

The first books Gutenberg produced were Bibles — 200 copies printed on vellum — which went on sale at the Frankfurt Book Fair in 1452. They sold for 300 florins each, a steep enough price at the time, but within the budget of most libraries and individuals in the rising middle class. Considering that at the time, Oxford's Bodleian Library contained a total of 122 manuscripts, each a priceless rarity, Gutenberg's Bible was affordable to all but the smallest libraries and the humblest of churches. By the year 1500, 2,500 European cities had Gutenberg presses and 8 million books had been printed. These included not only inexpensive translations of the Bible but also psalters (books of common prayer), scientific treatises, encyclopedias, herbals, bestiaries and volumes of poetry.

A printing press is like television or a computer, a work-related technology that has much wider implications, depending on how it is used. By itself, it simply makes the work of producing a book easier, faster and cheaper. But if certain kinds of books are printed on it, it has the potential to wrest knowledge and information from the control of a few and make them available to the many. With the printing press, words on paper became a means of influencing and directing the masses. When Martin Luther launched the Protestant Reformation by proclaiming, in 1517, that every Christian should be able to read the Bible, he wasn't thinking that everyone should have access to hand-copied, illuminated Latin manuscripts. He meant that even the meanest of sinners should have access to salvation through a Bible like Gutenberg's, printed in his or her own language. Thus technology enabled not only secular but religious reform. As John Man, Luther's biographer, puts it, "the noises that accompanied Luther's message . . . were probably not hammer-blows; they were the squeaks and bangs of busy printing presses."[3]

Another Renaissance precursor to the Industrial Revolution was the breaking down of the power of the guilds. The guild system, in which knowledge of specific crafts — goldsmithing, leatherworking, glassmaking, stonecutting — was jealously confined to members of the respective guild, had been established during the Middle Ages. In a way, the guild system was an early form of modern trade unionism: no one but a paid-up guild member was allowed to perform tasks controlled by that guild. The Renaissance, by contrast, was an age of generalization. The Renaissance craftsperson was a figure, as Lewis Mumford has observed, who "was equally ready to paint a picture, cast a bronze, plan a fortification, design a pageant, or construct a building."[4] This was the opposite of the medieval guildsman, who knew little outside his own specialized craft and was prevented by law from practicing a trade belonging to a guild of which he was not a member. As late as 1561, for instance, Hans Spaichl, a Nuremburg member of the red-metal turners guild, which oversaw the production of copper goods turned on lathes, invented a new type of lathe capable of producing finer work. When he lent his lathe to a goldsmith, the red-metal turners guild seized it and smashed it to pieces. New inventions were the property of the guild, not of the inventor, and nothing belonging to one guild could be used by another.

Printing changed all that. In fact, printing and the dissemination of knowledge weakened the whole notion of collectivity, whether related to guilds or to the Church, that had dominated previous centuries. It introduced the idea of individualism, a philosophical concept that led to the Industrial Revolution. Just as Martin Luther's Protestant Reformation emphasized the individual worshipper's relationship to the deity over the collective power of the Church — a Protestant could have a one-on-one relationship with God, whereas a Catholic had to appeal to God through intermediaries such as priests and saints — so the spread of arcane knowledge, through books and treatises, allowed individual craftspeople to obtain and use information that could no longer be controlled and confined by the guilds. This change had huge ramifications. For one thing, the concept of Romanticism that pervaded the nineteenth century is based on the celebration of the individual, which is the basis of capitalism and democracy. It became acceptable for an individual, say a factory owner, to profit from the work of the masses. As capitalists became more important to the efficient running of society, the role of the monarch was diminished, giving rise to the spirit, if not the letter, of democracy. As Thomas Carlyle would write two centuries later, "He who first shortened the labor of copyists by the device of Movable Type was disbanding hired armies, and cashiering most Kings and Senates, and creating a whole new democratic order."[5]

It was partly to break the power of the guilds that, toward the end of the sixteenth century, European countries instituted the notion of "privileges" to protect the right of inventors and manufacturers from having their inventions imitated by competitors or absorbed by guilds. We still have these privileges today; they're called patents. The granting of privileges produced a tidal wave of technological inventions and practices that further transformed society, preparing the way for individual advancement and competition. Wade Davis remarks in *The Wayfinders*, his book about the loss of ancient wisdom, that freeing the individual from the collective during the Renaissance "was the sociological equivalent of splitting the atom."[6]

Technological advances made during the Renaissance also made possible the practice of mass production. Many objects that in earlier times had been handmade by trained craftspersons, with a single craftsperson completing each object from start to finish, were now produced by semi-skilled workers in factory-like settings. In *De la pirotechnia*, Biringuccio describes a bronze foundry in Milan in which some workers would spend an entire day pouring molten bronze into molds to make "an infinite number" of buckles. The next day they would make nothing but chain links, the next day it would be harness bells or thimbles or window fasteners. This foundry and others — Biringuccio mentions similar operations in Flanders, Cologne and Paris — were the precursors of Henry Ford's assembly line. In an interesting confusion of imagery, Biringuccio writes that "whoever entered that shop and saw the activity of so many persons would, I think, believe, as I did, that he had entered an Inferno, nay, on the contrary, a Paradise, where there was a mirror in which sparkled all the beauty of genius and the power of art."[7] But which was it: Inferno or Paradise? Perhaps a Paradise for the foundry owner, but an Inferno for the workers stoking the fires and pouring the molten metal. Only the owner was a guildsman; the workers were unskilled, truly cogs in the great wheel known as mass production. The breakdown of the guilds and the establishment of mass production would lead, by the end of the eighteenth century, to the factory, an institution that functioned as a huge machine in which human beings were among the moving parts.

The establishment of a machine economy depended upon there first being a machine psychology. It was the French mathematician René Descartes (1596-1650), known as the founder of modern philosophy, who first proposed that everything in nature, from the growth of a tree to the movement of the planets, was mechanical and could be explained by mathematical formulae. Reviving the ancient Greek concept of dualism — that the human mind and the human body were separate, the mind linked directly with the divine and the body unfortunately tethered to the mundane Earth — Descartes also thought of the body as a machine that functioned independently of the mind. If I put my hand over a flame, for example, my arm jerks it away without any signal from my brain telling it to do so. "I should like you to consider," he wrote in *A Treatise on Man*, "that these functions . . . follow from the mere arrangement of the machine's organs every bit as naturally as the movements of a clock or other automatons follow from the arrangement of its counterweights and wheels." The body was a machine, "opposed to reason," and its movements could therefore be accounted for mathematically. The only difference between a human being and Vaucanson's mechanical duck, in other words, was that a human being could think.

Descartes' principle work, *A Discourse on Method*, published in 1637, effectively divided the world into two arenas: that of the intellect and that of the passions. The latter hindered the former, and it was the former — the human intellect — that made progress possible. And since progress was what human beings had been put on Earth to make, the passions had to be controlled. "Even those who have the feeblest souls can acquire a very absolute dominion over all their passions," wrote Descartes, "if sufficient industry is applied in training and guiding them." Industry. Absolute dominion. That was Descartes' "method": eliminate all emotion, all evidence of the senses, all compassion from human discourse, and progress toward perfection would be achieved. The theoretical roots of the Industrial Revolution and the centuries that have followed it are found in the cerebral ruminations of the man who first uttered the words, *"Je pense, donc je suis"* (I think, therefore I am).

Three centuries later, the conflict between the emotions and the intellect in individuals would be described by Sigmund Freud, the father of modern psychology, as a form of mental illness leading to a psychotic breakdown. Freud believed that schizophrenia, for example, was caused by a split between our emotional need to be close to our natures and our intellectual, or civilized, need to follow social conventions. In the seventeenth century, however, Descartes' ideas formed the basis for the Age of Reason, which became, in the eighteenth century, the Age of Enlightenment, culminating in the French and American Revolutions. The focus on individual achievement, the notion of inevitable progress, the ideal of mechanical perfection also led to the Industrial Revolution — a nightmarish time that can be described as a psychotic breakdown at the societal level.

Chapter 4
The Industrial Revolution

Revolutions, like psychoses, usually have specific dates of onset and root causes that stretch far back in time. However, it is difficult to pin an exact date on the start of the Industrial Revolution. In a sense, it was more evolution than revolution, because its industrial roots were in Renaissance metalworking factories and its philosophical bases were to be found in the writings of Descartes and other philosophers such as John Locke and Emannuel Kant. But there are a number of possible dates, each of which has to do with the invention, improvement or application of the steam engine. The list has a kind of *Sorcerer's Apprentice* quality to it that makes it seem like the unstoppable march of progress.

1712: Ironmonger and Baptist preacher Thomas Newcomen installs an "atmospheric engine" to draw water from the Conygree Coalworks in England's West Midlands. The engine, little more than a steam-driven mechanical pump, is extremely inefficient (it guzzles coal at the rate of about five tons per day). Nonetheless, seventy-five Newcomen engines are built during its inventor's lifetime, throughout Britain and eventually on the continent.

1733: Newcomen's patent expires, opening the field for others to improve on his original idea.

1769: Scottish machinist James Watt is granted a patent for "a new method of lessening the consumption of steam and fuel in fire engines."[1] A few years earlier, when Watt was repairing a Newcomen engine for the University of Glasgow, he realized that its main problem was that steam condensed back into water inside the cylinder, so the cylinder had to be reheated between each stroke of the piston. Watt thought the cylinder should remain at a high temperature, and that the steam should be directed through a valve into a condenser outside the main engine.

1772: John Smeaton installs Newcomen engines at the Long Benton colliery, in Northumberland, with a 132-centimeter (52-inch) diameter cylinder, and at Chacewater, Cornwall, with a 183-centimeter (72-inch) cylinder. Although they achieve only a 1 percent efficiency rate, they double the efficiency of Newcomen's original and become the main steam engine used throughout England and the continent for many years. It is Smeaton's version of Newcomen's engine, not Watt's improvement of it, that allows Great Britain to expand its coal-mining operations to the point at which the Industrial Revolution is possible.

1774: Richard Arkwright, an English wig maker, notices that although England's major natural resource is wool, the country's hand-loom weavers aren't keeping up with the demand for cloth because hand spinners can't supply them with enough yarn. He invents a machine for spinning yarn more quickly, using water power to turn the spinner wheels. By 1790, there are 155 yarn manufactories in England equipped with Arkwright's new "water frame," with a total of 310,000 spindles.

1781: Watt, who has teamed up with Matthew Boulton, a manufacturer and entrepreneur, builds two engines, one to pump water out of a colliery and another to pump air into a blast furnace. Both engines use a third of the amount of coal used by Newcomen's engine. At Boulton's suggestion, Watt has redesigned his engine to turn a crankshaft, opening up the enormous potential of the steam engine. Watt's smooth-running, precision-tooled machine will do much more than simply make a pump handle go up and down — it can be used to turn a wheel.

1784: Edward Cartwright, a Leicestershire rector, visits one of Arkwright's spinning mills in Manchester and discovers that the mills are now producing more yarn than the country's hand-loom weavers can handle. Cartwright sets about inventing a new automated loom that will increase the production of cloth. His "power loom," patented in 1785, incorporates Watt's double-action steam engine and is so efficient it soon replaces most of the operations formerly performed by humans with mechanical ones. Whereas a weaver working on a hand loom in her cottage could make only a few "picks," or passes, of the shuttle per minute, with Cartwright's loom, a single weaver — usually a man — working in a centralized factory can operate six power looms at a time, with flying shuttles making up to 260 picks per minute. By 1803, there are 2,400 power looms in operation in Great Britain; by 1857, there are 250,000.

This was progress, of a kind. But what is progress? It is, first of all, a European concept. Economist William Woodruff wrote in 1966 that "the idea of a continuous, cumulative expansion of man's power over his own environment . . . most sharply distinguishes the European from other civilizations. It is the most powerful idea that Europe has put abroad."[2]

The fact that other, perhaps greater, civilizations have rejected the notion of relentless progress toward some ill-defined goal of perfectionism ought perhaps to have given Western thinkers pause, but it didn't. China, for example, was far more technologically advanced, and far earlier, than Europe. In fact, there is some evidence that Renaissance Europe "received" many of its technological advances directly from the Chinese in 1434, when a huge fleet of Chinese ships sailed into the Mediterranean laden with many items unknown in Europe at the time: tilt and trip hammers, winnowing fans, bellows powered by piston rods, vertical water wheels for driving textile machinery, pearl-diving apparatus and the compass.[3] But the Chinese placed individual accomplishment and personal pleasure above notions of progress. Like the ancient Greeks — who had a form of water clock known as the "outflow clepsydra," but used it only in places where time had to be strictly regulated, such as in courtrooms and brothels — the Chinese used technology to enhance intellectual and artistic appreciation. For example, one Chinese inventor spent twenty years building a four-story mechanical clock run by a rotating water wheel that did little more than display the phases of the moon and the position of the constellations. He built it for amusement, not enlightenment. And Japan totally rejected Western technology, especially in the form of firearms, banning them from the nation from the sixteenth until the middle of the nineteenth centuries, because the prospect of the power of the samurai diminished by hordes of peasants bearing flintlocks did not, in their view, constitute "progress."

Not only is this notion of progress a European — and, by extension, a North American — phenomenon, it is also a relatively recent one. Physicist and novelist Alan Lightman reckons it is less than 300 years old, and connects it with the Industrial Revolution. Sometime in the early eighteenth century, he writes, "the development of technology became part of a major Western theme called 'progress' . . . Human beings were inevitably advancing to a higher plane — socially, politically, intellectually, scientifically, and morally."[4] The word "progress" existed before the technological boom, of course, but it had a humbler meaning. Progress was simply forward motion: the sun progressed across the sky, the queen made a progression from Paris to Versailles. But the sun did not become brighter as it progressed in the firmament; the queen did not become a better monarch in Versailles than she had been in Paris. Progress was not the same as improvement.

But during the Age of Reason, progress was understood as a movement toward enlightenment. In 1795, the French philosopher Nicolas de Condorcet suggested, in *Sketch for a Historical Picture of the Intellectual Progress of Mankind*, that the human race was "infinitely perfectible" and moving steadily toward the best of all possible worlds. His contemporary and colleague François-Marie Arouet de Voltaire saw science and reason as the main thrusts in the steady improvement of society. Conquering the passions, discounting the distortions and biases of the senses, organizing the world into neat, rational categories became inextricably linked with the advance of technology. Mineral, vegetable, animal; Negroid, Mongoloid, Caucasian — each rung up the ladder bringing humans closer to the European ideal of "perfection." Despite the evidence of the senses — crushing poverty, social demoralization, urban squalor, family disintegration — the Industrial Revolution was a good thing, because it brought great wealth to the nation and to the few individuals who controlled it.[5]

Even better, technology eliminated human frailty and error. In *The Philosophy of Manufactures*, published in 1835, Andrew Ure, a Scottish chemist who also lectured in mechanics in Glasgow, welcomed the onrush of "the British system of industry," in which every aspect of manufacture that had once been carried out by human workers was now "placed under the guidance of self-acting machinery." It almost sounds as though Ure were describing robots, a term that wouldn't appear until Karel Čapek's play *R.U.R.* (Rossum's Universal Robots) was first performed in 1921. But machines, like robots, are not "self-acting"; they are put into motion by human beings. Once they are activated, they *seem* to be self-perpetuating. It is easy to think of them as having minds and wills of their own, and functioning best without human interference. Ure wrote that "the most perfect manufacture is that which dispenses entirely with manual labor," and even attributed to machines a kind of consciousness: "It is in a cotton mill that the perfection of automatic industry is to be seen; it is there that the elemental powers have been made to animate millions of complex organs, infusing into forms of wood, iron, and brass an intelligent agency."[6]

At first, the mechanization of industry was universally viewed as an unalloyed boon, a sign of progress. Proponents placed great emphasis on speed and efficiency, which are the only things a machine can guarantee, and turned a blind eye to the decline in health and prosperity of individual workers, and to the loss of what Lightman calls "the inner self," meaning the part of us that indulges in contemplation, in simple enjoyment, and requires the leisure to enjoy the arts and nature.[7] In the early nineteenth century, the inner self meant the spiritual or religious life, and that, too, is what the Industrial Revolution eroded.

Mechanism had, at first, been encouraged by the Church, but when machines started replacing masses of workers, technology became a religion unto itself. In 1829, Thomas Carlyle, in the *Edinburgh Review*, noted that "this faith in Mechanism has now struck its roots down into man's most intimate, primary sources of conviction . . . The truth is, men have lost their belief in the Invisible, and believe, and hope, and work only in the Visible; or, to speak it in other words: This is not a Religious age. Only the material, the immediately practical, not the divine and spiritual, is important to us. The infinite, absolute character of Virtue has passed into a finite, conditional one; it is no longer a worship of the Beautiful and Good; but a calculation of the Profitable. Worship, indeed, in any sense, is not recognised among us, or is mechanically explained into Fear of pain, or Hope of pleasure. Our true Deity is Mechanism."[8]

Carlyle wasn't the first to sound the alarm against mechanism, but earlier protests had been less philosophical and therefore more easily put down. In 1779, a Leicestershire mill worker named Ned Ludd broke into a factory at night and smashed two machines used to knit stockings. He acted, one newspaper reported, "in a fit of insane rage," possibly after having been whipped for idleness, although it was more likely after having been fired as redundant. English mill owners had begun importing knitting frames from Germany that produced stockings and lace with fewer human hands, and consequently thousands of English textile workers were being thrown out of work. The new machines could produce six times the work of the older frames, and although the woolen material they produced was "shoddy" (a textile term that means wool produced from waste material, such as old rags, but having the appearance of high quality), mill owners continued to bring them in. The issue that most concerned laborers at the turn of the nineteenth century was not the decline of religion, but mass unemployment.

In November 1811, bands of hooded men began breaking into woolen mills throughout England, smashing machinery and burning bales of cloth, calling themselves followers of Ludd, or Luddites. Over a period of fourteen months, more than 1,100 knitting frames were destroyed. Police and eventually the army were called in; by May, there were 34,000 troops on alert, and Parliament had passed a law making the destruction of textile machinery a hanging offence. Not only were machines replacing people, they had become more valued than people. This was not a subtle shift; it was the true face of revolution.

The rioting went on. The rioters abstained from bloodshed, but in 1812 several frame breakers were shot by soldiers called in by a mill owner, who was subsequently found murdered. After a trial, ten Luddites were hanged, many were imprisoned, and thirty-eight were transported to penal colonies in Australia. The Luddites made some serious disturbances, but they had caused hardly a misstep in the steady march of the machine mentality. In fact, the ruthlessness with which the government put down the rebels only proved to mill owners that, when industrial progress was challenged, the government would back the mill owners, not the people. Industrialists had been given a green light to increase the number of factories, decrease the number of workers, lower wages and benefits, and further mechanize the manufacturing process. "The open alliance of government and industry," writes Kirkpatrick Sale, "laid bare the true nature of the state and its willingness to use any force at hand in service to industrialism." He might have written "in service to technology." It was a grim lesson, and set the tone for the rest of the nineteenth century and beyond. "The machinery question," as it was called, might have been answered in many ways, but with government supporting the industrialists, continues Sale, the message "was that all machines were legitimate and the economic and social consequences, however horrible, were irrelevant."[9]

Leo Marx, in *The Machine in the Garden* (1964), suggests that, at some point in the mid-nineteenth century, the perception of technology in Western society underwent a major shift. At the beginning of the Industrial Revolution it was still possible to argue that mechanization, though admittedly detrimental to some individuals, was unquestionably a boon to society at large. By about 1870 the emphasis had reversed: technology, though admittedly a boon to some individuals, was increasingly detrimental to society at large. Mechanization had progressed from a universal good to a necessary evil. Two developments underscore the turn technology took and the public's eventual reaction against it.

Because machines gave factory owners the ability to employ unskilled workers, the door was opened to child labor. Children were small, nimble, could be paid a fraction of an adult's wage and didn't rebel against poor working conditions as much as adults. The first manufacturers in England to employ children were two brothers, Job and William Wyatt, who opened the first machine-made screw factory in 1760. A quarter of a century later, nearly one-third of all workers in England's rural factories were "apprentices" under the age of fifteen, some of them as young as five. In industrialized cities such as Manchester, Birmingham and London, children were abundant as more and more families gave up agriculture and moved to urban centers to work in industry. The population of Manchester in 1760 was 30,000; by 1821 it was 187,000. During the same period, the population of London nearly doubled, rising from 750,000 to 1.4 million. By mid-century, one out of every two people living in Great Britain lived in London.

Aside from overcrowding and poor pay, working conditions in the mills were often dangerous and unhealthy, especially for children, whose developing bodies made them more vulnerable. In 1830, Robert Southey, England's poet laureate, described the textile industry as "a wen, a fungus excrescence from the body politic." Smog in the streets combined with cotton dust in the mills to create serious health problems. In France, British textile machinery imported in the 1820s turned the Lower Seine and Alsace districts into vast landscapes of mill stacks and poor housing, and working conditions became the focus of intense inquiry. Wealthy industrialists were able to move into the country, but the poor had to stay where the machines were, and their physical and mental health suffered for it.

In 1840, Louis-René Villermé, a doctor in the city of Mulhouse, France, described textile factories in which children as young as four and a half worked twelve-hour days alongside adults, washing bobbins, tying broken threads, sweeping floors, applying dyes to dye-plates and always breathing cotton dust. The factories, Villermé wrote, "are commonly built on bare ground, are dark, damp, and receive little or no air. Such locations are chosen deliberately, despite the effect on the workers' health, in order to maintain the suppleness, moisture content, elasticity, and strength of the thread."[10] Temperatures regularly rose to 40°C (104°F), and the windows were kept tightly shut so that no incoming breezes dried out the threads, making them more liable to break.

In 1834, factories in the Lower Seine employed 100,000 workers, one-third of them children. Malnourishment was apparent in their size and stooped comportment. The most common complaint was "the goiter," the swelling of the thyroid gland caused by lack of iodine. The main source of iodine, before iodized salt, was meat, and factory workers were living almost entirely on a diet of potatoes and bread, rarely eating meat more than twice a month. Genetic disorders abounded. In Britain's coal mines, where coal was still mined with picks and shovels, small children were employed to push carts through mine shafts too small to admit adults. If the children were too young for that, they opened the trap doors for the boys pushing the corves (baskets) of coal.

The first Factory Act in England, intended to regulate the age at which children could be hired and the maximum hours they could work, was passed in 1802, but proved ineffective. The problem was too complex to be solved by a simple act of parliament and, as the Luddite revolt would show, Parliament was more concerned with keeping the factories running than with the condition or age of the workers. In 1833, 57 percent of the employees in English textile mills were under the age of eighteen. That year, Lord Ashley, a member of the House of Commons, proposed a bill that would limit the working hours of children under twelve to ten hours a day, but it was defeated by a vote of 283 to 93. Parliament, however, later passed the second Factory Act, stating that children had to be nine years old to work in factories; children twelve and under could be made to work no more than eight hours a day; and children over thirteen could work twelve hours a day. This was an improvement, but not by much. Many of the children under nine who were now prevented from working in the factories were sent by their parents to work in the coal mines.[11]

Even poet Robert Southey agreed that there seemed

to be no solution to the horrors of child labor, which he compared to a cancer that had been detected too late. "The growth might have been checked," he wrote, "if the consequences had been apprehended in time; but now it has acquired so great a bulk, its nerves have branched so widely, and the vessels of the tumor are so inosculated into some of the principal veins and arteries of the natural system, that to remove it by absorption is impossible, and excision will be fatal."[12]

Whether we liked mechanism or not, it had come to stay. The wealth of the nation depended upon it, and, increasingly, people depended upon the wealth of the nation.

Meanwhile, the vessels of the tumor had spread to the United States, where the second objection to mechanization became manifest. It is ironic that mechanization was embraced in the Middle Ages because it made slavery unnecessary, whereas in America it was technology that made slavery inevitable.

The word "technology" with its current meaning is an Americanism. It came into the English language, from the Greek *tekhne*, meaning art, skill or method, in the early seventeenth century, but referred solely to the practice or study of grammar and the arts. American literary critic Louis Menand was quite right when he suggested that writing itself is a form of technology.

What we now call technology — the manufacture and maintenance of machines or systems to do work that was previously performed by humans — was referred to in former times as "the mechanical arts." In 1829, Harvard professor Jacob Bigelow revived the term, noting that "technology serves to extend the dominion of mankind over nature." Technology defined the difference between primitive and civilized societies: "The economy of the ancients," he wrote, "consisted in diminishing their personal wants; ours, in devising cheap means to gratify them." Bigelow suggested to William Barton Rogers, who in 1859 was casting about for a name for a new school in Boston that would teach the "arts of science," that he should call it the "Massachusetts Institute of Technology."[13]

The MIT version of technology had entered the US by means of a security leak. In 1789, Samuel Slater, an Englishman who had been apprenticed to a cotton-mill owner named Jebediah Strutt, the partner of Richard Arkwright, decided to start a cotton mill in New England. English law, however, forbade the exportation of textile machinery, or even drawings of it, so Slater memorized the design for one of Arkwright's water frames. After emigrating to America, he joined with businessman Moses Brown to build a textile mill in Pawtucket, Rhode Island, which began production in 1790.

In 1774, Richard Arkwright had persuaded the British Parliament to repeal the Calico Act of 1721, which protected British wool and linen industries by prohibiting the manufacture, sale or even the wearing of cotton. Villains who were publicly hanged in England were dressed in cotton garments, just to give the cloth a bad name. With the Calico Act suspended, cotton importation into England shot from zero to 6.7 million pounds a year by 1780. The cotton came from India (the word "calico" comes from the old name for Calcutta) and the Middle East ("muslin" is a corruption of Moussoul, or Mosul, a cotton-producing city in what is now central Iraq). Soon after Slater's mill opened, however, it started coming in ever-increasing quantities from the United States.

The power loom came to the United States in a similarly underhanded way, via Francis Cabot Lowell, of the prosperous Lowell family of Boston. Lowell traveled to Manchester, England, in 1810 to study the British textile industry. Like Slater, he memorized plans for Cartwright's power loom. Back in the US, he hired a mechanic named Paul Moody to construct a factory in Waltham, Massachusetts, that would include every stage of cotton production from raw cotton to cloth. Lowell was the first industrialist to hire women: his "mill girls," or "Lowell girls," as they came to be called, were as young as fifteen, and lived in dormitories where they were paid less than men, but were fed, clothed and chaperoned.

When Slater opened his spinning factory in 1790, the cotton he spun came from the state of Georgia, and the seeds had to be cleaned from it by hand. Hand-cleaning was a laborious process. It took one slave an entire day to clean one pound of cotton. In 1792, a northerner named Eli Whitney, who was teaching school in Georgia, came up with an idea for cleaning cotton mechanically. He called his invention a cotton gin, or "saw-gin" ("gin" being short for "engine"). It consisted of two wooden cylinders spinning in opposite directions. Saw blades on the surface of the smaller cylinder caught the cotton and forced it between brushes on the larger cylinder, and the brushes picked out the cotton seeds. It seemed simple enough, perhaps too simple. Although Whitney applied for a patent in 1794, he didn't receive it until 1807, by which time his saw-gin had been copied so often that he had been bankrupt since 1797. Every Southern plantation had a cotton gin, but few of them had been purchased from Whitney.

With a cotton gin, one slave could clean 25 kilograms (55 pounds) of raw cotton per day. When the gin was attached to a steam engine, a slave could clean 453 kilograms (1,000 pounds) or a full bale of cotton a day. Almost overnight, cotton production in the American South skyrocketed. In 1790, the entire US production of raw cotton was 3,135 bales. In 1810, production leapt to 177,638 bales. By 1825, the United States was producing more than half a million bales and was supplying more than 80 percent of the world's cotton, not only to Great Britain but to the rapidly increasing number of textile mills in the northern United States, all of which were mechanized. Some were run by water mills, but many were powered by steam.

American historian Herbert Aptheker, author of *A Documentary History of the Negro People in the United States*, suggests that Eli Whitney copied the design for his cotton gin from a drawing made by a slave in Mississippi. If true, it would be one of the supreme ironies of the Industrial Revolution, because the cotton gin made the US the world's biggest cotton producer and, as a consequence, the largest importer of slaves in the world. In 1790, there were 700,000 slaves in the United States; in 1860, on the eve of the Civil War, when America produced 3.8 billion pounds of cotton, the number of slaves had risen to nearly 4 million, with 70 percent of them working in cotton production in the Deep South. In the southern cotton-producing states of Virginia, Georgia, the Carolinas, Mississippi and Alabama, slaves made up 45 percent of the total population.

It was the advent of technology that led to the increase in and prolongation of slavery in the US, where the right to own slaves was enshrined in the Declaration of Independence and not rescinded until 1865, thirty-two years after slavery had been abolished in the British Empire.

The opening of the first World's Fair in London on May 1, 1851, signaled the beginning of the end of technology's hold on Europe, and the beginning of its appeal in the United States. Called the Great Exhibition of the Works of Industry of all Nations, it was located in Hyde Park. The Crystal Palace, a massive iron-and-glass testament to industrial design, had been constructed in nine months to accommodate 13,000 exhibits intended to showcase the century's major accomplishments in the fields of agriculture and manufacture. Exhibitors came from Britain, Europe, India, Australia, New Zealand and the United States. Six million visitors paid their shilling to view such diverse inventions as the daguerreotype, Walter Hunt's sewing machine, the Jacquard loom, the McCormick reaper, Cooke's and Wheatstone's electromagnetic telegraph, Hobbs's door locks, a voting machine, Crampton's Patent Express railway locomotive, and mass-produced silverware, glassware and other household items. The fair was a way of showing the world the legacy that the Industrial Revolution had left to England: a healthy industry, a vibrant nation, and what one observer has called "the technical materialism of modernity."[14]

But even as the fair-goers were gazing wide-eyed at the world's technology, rumblings against the purely mechanized world they were viewing were being heard in Europe, this time not only from the workers who were cast out of jobs, but from intellectuals who foresaw the loss of the natural, spontaneous, non-automated world of nature. In 1850, Alfred Tennyson, the great, portentous poet of the Victorian era, published "In Memoriam," an elegy for his friend Arthur Hallam, but also a lament for the loss of all that was young and regenerative. The poem portrayed a stark picture of contemporary England in which Death stalked the countryside, and once verdant meadows and forests had been turned into towns and factories, and people into mindless automatons:

I dream'd there would be Spring no more,
    That Nature's ancient power was lost:
    The streets were black with smoke and frost,
They chatter'd trifles at the door.

Even William Wordsworth, who had grown up during the height of the Industrial Revolution, had written that "the world is too much with us," and that we dedicate far too much time to "getting and spending."[15]

The two most powerful critiques of technology, however, came later in the century. One looked back over two centuries of increasing mechanization and simply rejected them; the other looked ahead to a technological future in which human beings were reduced to ciphers and called for a return to human dignity and meaning.

The first was Samuel Butler's utopian novel, *Erewhon*, in which an English traveler in New Zealand stumbles into a hidden valley and finds an entire society living in seclusion from the outside world; the people in it have outlawed any invention that came after 1600. Butler had become alarmed at the degree to which Victorians were dependent on machines: "If all machines were to be annihilated at one moment," he wrote, "and if all knowledge of mechanical laws were taken from him so that he could make no more machines, and all machine-made food destroyed so that the race of man should be left as it were naked upon a desert island, we should become extinct in six weeks."[16] In Erewhon, machines had not been allowed to take that stranglehold on humanity, and the society was thriving — at least until the Englishman entered it.

The other, forward-looking book was destined to become one of the most influential works of all time: Karl Marx's first volume of *Das Kapital,* published in 1867. Marx saw that what was emerging in a highly technological, largely depersonalized society were increasingly complex systems, like factories and railroads, that were hugely profitable for a handful of individuals but demoralizing and dehumanizing for the rest of society. His masterwork was a critique not so much of technology as of the capitalists and technocrats who controlled it, because technology in the wrong hands turned capitalism into an oppressive system. If workers rather than owners could manage to control the means of production, Marx maintained, something like Butler's Erewhon could exist in the real world.

Unfortunately for both Butler's and Marx's visions, it was too late. Technology could no longer be rejected; it had become a fact of life. And if technology was going to be controlled, it wasn't the workers who were going to control it.

Chapter 5
Modern Times

As the effect of technology on life and art was being questioned in Europe, the US was welcoming ever newer technology with open arms. "Consider the [mechanical] arts . . . as illustrating the mind of God," enthused an 1857 editorial in *Harper's Magazine*, echoing Church fathers of the fourteenth century and once again yoking technology with religion. "Industry," the editorial continued, "is the champion of freedom and order."[1] As historian Perry Miller has observed, Americans at the end of the nineteenth century "flung themselves into the technological torrent; how they shouted with glee in the midst of the cataract, and cried to each other, as they went headlong down the chute, that here was their destiny."[2]

Once technology is linked to progress — any advance in technology equals an advance in civilization — its nature shifts dramatically. The stakes go up. Simple work-related technologies, such as the telephone, the word processor or the automobile, are no longer good enough in themselves but must be further developed into a controlled system. In

American Genesis: A Century of Invention and Technological Enthusiasm, Thomas P. Hughes provides a new definition of technology as "the effort to organize the world for problem solving so that goods and services can be invented, developed, produced, and used."[3] If any one phrase characterizes the modern US, it is "the effort to organize the world," and that effort is clearly derived from the nation's embracing of industry.

At first, few of the technological inventions that transformed the United States from a hinterland of raw materials to an industrialized superpower originated in North America. Just as much of the technology that characterized Europe's Middle Ages and Renaissance came from China, so most of the technology that animated the United States came from Europe. The 1857 *Harper's* editorialist named three "heroes" of innovation — Martin Luther, Christopher Columbus and Johann Gutenberg, "representing severally the opened Bible, the New World, the Printing-Press, powers that have brought all progress in their train."[4] None of them were Americans, but the cast was soon to be supported by Thomas Edison, Henry Ford and Alexander Graham Bell. The starring role of the United States was to take ideas from Europe and transplant them in the New World, where they would take off like kudzu.

The sewing machine, for example, was invented in 1830 by the French engineer Barthélemy Thimonnier, who manufactured eighty of them. In an episode reminiscent of the Luddite uprisings in England, all eighty machines were destroyed by a mob of angry tailors fearful of being put out of work by technology. No such outrage greeted Elias Howe's sewing machine in the US, however. In fact, Howe's design, patented in 1854, was copied by Isaac Singer, who paid Howe more than $2 million in royalties until Howe's patent expired in 1867. In the US, the sewing machine was hailed as technology that liberated the nascent seamstress who lurked in all women, allowing them to work at home instead of in sweatshops, or to make their own clothes rather than buying them in dress shops.

But as Freeman Dyson points out, "a step forward in technology tends to bring with it an unexpected step backward." To put it another way, an advance in work-related technology tends to lead to a furtherance in control-related technological thinking. In the case of household appliances, such as dishwashers, electric irons, stoves and sewing machines, the step backward has been primarily forced upon middle-class women. Women who had once had domestic servants to do the housework, leaving them free to pursue their interests outside the home, were now expected to find housework faster and less expensive if they got rid of the servants and did the work themselves. Women "liberated" by technology ended up cooking, cleaning the house, looking after the children, doing laundry and even sewing their family's clothes, all of which confined them to the home. It took more than half a century for women to gain back the personal freedom they had enjoyed in the nineteenth century, and even then, "to achieve even partial liberation," Dyson writes, women "have replaced the old domestic servants with day-care centers, cleaning ladies, and au pair girls imported from overseas."[5]

Photography was also a French invention. In 1826, Joseph Nicéphore Niépce produced the world's first photograph on paper using a process that required exposure times of up to eight hours and was therefore practical only for photographing buildings and landscapes. In 1839, French theater designer Louis-Jacques-Mandé Daguerre patented a process that reduced exposures to under thirty minutes, making it possible to photograph people, provided they could sit still for half an hour.

Frederick Scott Archer's "wet-plate" process came along in 1851. A glass plate was coated with a mixture of collodion (gun-cotton dissolved in ether) and potassium iodide, and then dipped in a silver nitrate solution. Traveling photographers required a dark-tent, a whole laboratory of chemicals and a large camera on a tripod, with the familiar black hood under which the photographer stood to focus on the subject. The equipment weighed 54 kilograms (120 pounds). In 1871, the English chemist Richard Leach Maddox perfected a "dry-plate" technique using a gelatin emulsion that took an image twenty times faster than collodion. Because "faster" had already become "better," by 1880 there were fourteen companies in England producing dry plates for sale. The era of the amateur photographer had dawned, and with it the public fascination with the photographic image.

There remained one more step, however, before the camera could become the household item it is today. That step was taken in the United States, in 1888, when John Wesley Hyatt of Newark, New Jersey, developed a method for producing thin, clear sheets of a kind of plastic he called Celluloid. Sheets of clear Celluloid were coated with Maddox's gelatin emulsion, and the new "film" replaced glass plates, which meant that film could be cut into strips and rolled.

The following year, George Eastman patented the first Kodak camera, which could take a hundred photographs per roll of film. If faster was better, faster and easier was better still. Eastman's customers took their photos, sent the camera to the Eastman Company, which developed the film, reloaded the camera, and returned both to the customer. This was essentially the photographic process that dominated the industry for the next century, until the invention of the digital camera in 1985.

The camera is not a negative piece of technology in itself, but it has had negative applications and consequences. In the hands of a skilled artist, a photograph can be a work of art equal in impact to any painting. But the ubiquity of the camera and its derivatives, the motion-picture camera and the video-camera recorder or camcorder, have led to such a proliferation of images that some social scientists now fear that images of an event have become more important to us — even more real to us — than the event itself. At a recent jazz concert in which the musicians were performing live with their performance simultaneously broadcast on a huge Jumbotron located immediately beside the stage, I noticed that at least half the audience was watching the Jumbotron instead of the live musicians.

A more disturbing example is our willingness to hand over decisions to machines. In a baseball game played in June 2010, a pitcher was on the threshold of pitching a perfect game, the rarest event in baseball: eight and two-thirds innings in which he had allowed no hits, no runs and no errors. In the bottom of the ninth inning, the first-base umpire called a runner safe who was clearly shown in video replays to have been out. Even the umpire admitted after the game that he had made a mistake. The pitcher had lost his perfect game due to human error — an umpire's bad call. Not only were there requests that the Commissioner of Baseball reverse the umpire's decision and award the pitcher his perfect game, there was even talk of eliminating human umpires altogether, and letting games be decided entirely by machines — as many professional tennis games and most Olympic events already are. Similar appeals were heard after disputed goals during the 2010 World Cup soccer tournament in South Africa. We seem to want to increase our reliance on technology rather than diminish it.

The tendency to believe communication images more than our own senses has huge political implications. Ursula Franklin finds that our reliance on image over reality has "so completely changed the real world of technology that we now live in a world that is *fundamentally* different." The war in Iraq, for instance, was more familiar to most North Americans through televised images of it than by direct experience, even though it was known that those televised images were almost completely controlled by the US government. We watched the war as we would watch a Hollywood movie and took away from it what the directors wanted us to take. Moreover, "the faraway that cannot be assessed through experience," writes Franklin, like the war in Iraq, "has *preference* over the near that can be experienced directly."[6] Events in Afghanistan, for instance, assume greater importance and are more real to us than events at home, such as increases in unemployment, cuts to social services and the arts, or the erosion of parliamentary democracy, because we can watch them on television. As in Orwell's *Nineteen Eighty-Four*, a determined government can bombard us with technologically manipulated images of its success in order to distract us from more tangible indications of its failure.

The internal combustion engine was a European invention. The first was built by Belgian inventor Étienne Lenoir in 1859. Lenoir adapted a double-acting steam engine to run on coal gas — a mixture of hydrogen, methane and carbon monoxide — and air ignited by an electric spark. Although not very efficient, it was small and lightweight compared to steam engines, and pointed to intriguing possibilities. In 1862, for instance, Lenoir installed one of his engines in the first "automobile," and drove it 10 kilometers (6 miles), a trip that consumed 3 hours and 8.5 cubic meters (300 cubic feet) of coal gas.

The first gasoline engine was patented by German inventor Gottlieb Daimler in 1884. Air was bubbled through a carburetor two-thirds full of gasoline, sucked into the cylinder and ignited by an electric spark. Five years later, Daimler built the first two-cylinder engine, which achieved such a high speed of rotation, up to 900 revolutions per minute compared to 80 to 150 for the gas engine, that it was quickly adopted by other manufacturers. One of these was Karl Benz, who in 1885 built a three-wheeled vehicle with a single-cylinder petrol engine and a vertical crankshaft capable of traveling 13 kilometers (8 miles) per hour. He later modified the design by making the crankshaft horizontal, and hundreds of models were produced. In 1893, he patented a four-wheeled motorcar with a Daimler engine and later formed the Cannstatt-Daimler company, which produced vehicles that eventually became known as Mercedes.

In other countries, similar motorcars were produced, in England by Lord Austin, and in France by Armand Peugeot and the Renault Brothers. By the turn of the century, motorcars with front-mounted engines, three gears, steering wheels (instead of tillers) and pneumatic tires were achieving speeds of 32 kilometers (20 miles) per hour in races conducted by the Automobile Club of Great Britain and Ireland.

American inventors like Thomas Edison, Henry Ford and the Wright brothers took European inventions and turned them into mass-produced items, not for the rich or the idle, but for the masses. The Wright brothers were the first to get an airplane off the ground, but the notion of heavier-than-air flying machines had been tried in Europe for decades. Edison opened his "invention factories" in Menlo Park, California, and West Orange, New Jersey, and by 1886 was working on, among many other things, motorcars and a system of electric lighting that had also been conceived in Europe. Henry Ford was Edison's chief engineer in 1893, and began tinkering with motorcars himself. With Edison's support, he built a four-wheeled "Quadricycle" that had a Daimler engine, ran on solid rubber tires and could travel up to 48 kilometers (30 miles) per hour. Still not satisfied, he quit Edison's and started the Ford Motor Company, in Detroit, and in 1908 issued the first Model T Ford, which had a four-cylinder, 20-horsepower engine capable of traveling 72 kilometers (45 miles) per hour. So successful was this model that between 1908 and 1927 the company produced 15 million Model Ts with no major design changes.

What did change, however, was the method of producing the cars. Ford's innovative production technique is a perfect example of control-based technology. For the first few years, each car was individually assembled by a team of two or three skilled mechanics capable of assembling only eleven cars in a month. In 1913, however, Ford introduced the "assembly line" system, in which each car was assembled by a line of eighty-four workers, each of whom was responsible for only one small part of the entire operation. This "division of labor," which had been put into practice by English textile manufacturers a hundred years previously (and by Italian metalworkers a hundred years before that), allowed Ford to cut manufacturing costs by hiring unskilled workers, with only a small group of overseers who needed to understand the construction of an entire car. In the 1920s, when Ford built his $240-million, 0.6-million-square-meter (7-million-square-foot) plant in Dearborn, 81,000 workers were assembling Model Ts so quickly that a new car rolled off the assembly line every three minutes. Henry Ford was to the automobile what Richard Arkwright had been to cotton cloth.

In 1911, two years before Ford introduced the assembly line, the American social theorist Frederick Winslow Taylor had published *The Principles of Scientific Management*, which became the textbook of the Efficiency Movement of the 1920s and 1930s. Shops across the United States adopted Taylor's efficient methods of production, schools and universities introduced efficiency into their curricula, and government agencies began using Taylor's criteria for efficiency in project assessments. Taylor's ideas sought to realize Andrew Ure's dream of turning factories into big, efficient machines, with unskilled laborers as insignificant cogs in the wheel. "All possible brain work should be removed from the shop," Taylor wrote, "and centered in the planning or layout department."[7]

Taylorism, as it was called, created several social problems. The changes Taylor advocated were not in the interest of increased quality or even better efficiency, but of lower labor costs. Less skilled workers could be paid less, resulting in increased poverty among worker families. Second, such "efficiency" resulted in a labor force that felt it was doing work that was not valued by society. While consumers may have placed a high value on a motorcar, they did not think that the ability to install a door handle or turn a tire lug required much skill or intelligence. Where once workers had taken pride in their accomplishment, they now felt belittled and ashamed of what they did for a living. Third, turning a factory into a well-oiled machine resulted in high unemployment, particularly among skilled workers. In 1900, there were 7,632 wagon and carriage manufacturers in the United States. After Ford's methods were adapted by other manufacturers, who had to compete with Ford's output, the industry was reduced to three: Ford, General Motors and Chrysler. Within decades, an entire skill set had vanished.

What Henry Ford and later industrialists created was the technological system, a way of turning not only factories but also entire environments into metaphorical machines. The groundwork for these sprawling systems had been laid in Europe, where vast railway and telegraph networks linked distant places and people in ways that had never been experienced before. In America, these networks quickly spread into virtually all walks of life. "Large systems," writes Thomas Hughes, "compose the essence of modern technology." Hughes cites energy, communication and transportation systems as quintessentially American phenomena: Americans, he writes, "might well see the 'system' as their hallmark."[8]

The Ford Motor Company was simply the most graspable of the new systems; people understood how cars were made. But gradually, more and more complex systems came into play. The sudden ubiquity of automobiles led to a high demand for gasoline, for example, the supply of which required vast petroleum refining systems, service stations and transportation networks. At the turn of the twentieth century, gasoline was a by-product of kerosene, essentially a waste product. By 1913, a new method of getting more gasoline from oil had been developed by the Standard Oil Company. Within five years, the Universal Oil Products Company introduced a continuous-feed process involving a sequence of processes (invented by a man whose name, believe it or not, was Carbon Petroleum Dubbs) that increased production and also improved gasoline quality, which meant that more cars could move faster. By 1924, engine noise was reduced by the addition of tetraethyl lead to gasoline. This process was the result of research by a network of concerns, including the Dow Chemical Company, General Motors, Du Pont Chemical, Standard Oil of New Jersey, Brown University and MIT.

Leaded gasoline is a good example of the way in which technological systems began to override human concerns: what was good for the system was assumed to be good for society. As soon as leaded gas was sold at the pumps by the Ethyl Gasoline Corporation — a new venture formed in 1924 by General Motors and Standard Oil — health authorities began to express concern about lead poisoning. The US Bureau of Mines exposed test animals to gas emissions for several hours a day for months and reported finding no sign of lead poisoning. In 1925, when forty-five people working at various oil refineries became ill, and four died, sales were halted and the US surgeon general ordered an investigation. Once again, the investigating committee found no cause for alarm. Sales resumed, and continued until leaded gasoline began to be phased out by higher tax measures in 1973, because of renewed health concerns. It wasn't officially banned in the US until the Clean Air Act of 1996, however, and even now is prohibited only in on-road vehicles. Leaded gas is still legal in airplanes, off-road vehicles, boat motors and farm equipment, and is still sold legally in many countries.

But was the lesson learned? Apparently not. A parallel situation exists today with genetically modified organisms (GMOs). To genetically modify a plant, biotechnicians take a gene responsible for a desired trait — say, the production of a protein that causes insects to lose their ability to digest food — from one organism (a bacterium) and transfer it into the genetic code of the host plant (say, corn) to produce a variety of corn that will cause corn-boring beetles to starve to death. They have, essentially, created a new life form, a product of nature theoretically modified to do exactly what we want it to do.

Traditional plant breeders have been producing hybridized varieties for centuries, but with genetic modification the new plant can be made virtually overnight rather than over a series of many plant generations. Moreover, hybrids can be made of organisms that, in nature, cannot share their genetic makeup (like bacteria and corn). Genetic modification can have moral or even political overtones, as in the recent attempt to create a poppy that produces codeine instead of morphine. (Heroin is synthesized from morphine, a derivative of opium, and 70 percent of the world's opium poppies are grown in Afghanistan.) But the aim is usually economic, since the traits most often selected for are herbicide and pesticide resistance.

Millions of acres of GM food plants are grown around the world, despite the fact that it is still unclear whether or not genetically modified food is safe for human consumption. Some scientists insist that it is not. According to biologist Barry Commoner, director of New York University's Critical Genetics Project, the potential for a GM seed to produce a protein that is dangerous to humans is "very real." Commoner was alerted to the danger of genetic modification when a Belgian lab found a scrambled section of DNA in GM soybeans that was not soybean DNA: the injected gene had produced an "unexpected" protein. When biotechnologists introduce foreign genes into an organism, they "disrupt the contextual relationship that exists between the gene and the rest of the cell." In other words, no one can foresee what new protein will be produced when a plant is genetically modified; two or three generations down the line, the plant may produce a protein that is toxic to humans.

When biotech companies release a GM plant into the marketplace, Commoner says, they are conducting a mass, uncontrolled experiment "using the whole world as a lab," and everyone in it as guinea pigs. "Even a low-probability mess-up is liable to occur," he says. The genetic modification of plants is a prime example of "technology doing things that science doesn't know."[9] Despite such warnings, biotech companies that produce GMOs and the governments that license them insist that the products are safe. Just as for fifty years all of the gasoline sold in the world was leaded, currently all of the soybeans and canola and most of the corn produced in North America are grown from genetically modified seeds. GM food has been banned in many European and several African countries, but it is extremely difficult to identify products made with GM ingredients such as corn syrup and soy oil.

In their 1999 book *The Technology Machine: How Manufacturing Will Work in the Year 2020*, Patricia Moody and Richard Morley predict that "technology, or machine intelligence, combined with individual excellence and integrity, will rule the future." They look forward to this future, in which the workforce will be divided into those who live on "Islands of Excellence" and the "nonelite group" of workers who have followed unprofitable pathways of manufacture, making such items as "flashlight switches, broiler pans, and vinyl dog collars." The "associates" on the islands will attend a "holistic, two-year apprenticeship program" and wear uniforms. "The first fifteen minutes of each day are spent in light exercise, a form of Tai Chi. Sometimes associates sing or participate in an island-wide assembly." The authors don't specify what these associates will manufacture on their islands, but they will be part of an "integration of spiritual energy with physical and mental capabilities."[10]

This vision, presented as a kind of Shangri-la of manufacturing, has decidedly nightmarish elements that make it more like Orwell's *Nineteen Eighty-Four* than like James Hilton's *Lost Horizons* (of Shangri-la fame). It represents "system" taken to its extreme, in which all individuality is subsumed into a mindless, faceless, integrated oneness. "Both sexes and many racial and ethnic 'colors,'" the authors write, will disappear: "From not too great a distance all personal differences blend into the overall design."[11] It doesn't seem to occur to Moody and Morley that many people don't want to blend into the design, that human beings are not robots. Moody and Morley are hailing a new Industrial Revolution, one that extols "metasystems" rather than mechanical innovations, but nonetheless relies on the sublimation of the many in order to realize the profit of the few.

No Islands of Excellence have appeared or are likely to appear by the year 2020, partly because people don't want them, and partly because technology moves in such multiple and unexpected directions that predicting the future is like shooting at an erratically moving target. This has ever been the case — in the 1840s, Karl

Marx predicted that capitalism was producing such a surplus of goods that it would soon crumple under its own weight. That hasn't happened yet. Instead, it was Marxism-inspired communism that collapsed. In 1985, when physicist Freeman Dyson was asked to predict the three most important developments of the twenty-first century, he listed genetic engineering, artificial intelligence — the development of robots that can think and act like humans — and space travel. Fifteen years later, as the twenty-first century dawned, he admitted that he had been wildly off in his predictions. Genetic engineering, the cloning of animals including humans, had stalled in its tracks; artificial intelligence is still a long way from coming up with anything more sophisticated than a superior telephone answering machine; and, as Dyson writes, "space travel is a joke."[12]

In 1999, Dyson made a new list. This time he predicted that the three most fruitful fields of technological endeavor in the first half of this century would be human genetics, solar energy and the Internet. With peak oil just around the corner and atomic energy failing to live up to its potential, it is a safe bet that alternative energy sources will make a strong showing in the next few decades. However, wind and water energy still rely on turning turbines, which is nineteenth-century technology. Solar energy captured by photovoltaic panels represents the only real technological advance in the energy field.

By human genetics, Dyson was thinking of the Human Genome Project, a major effort by the US

Department of Energy and the National Institutes of Health, begun in 1990, with the goal of identifying each of our 20,000 to 25,000 genes to determine the sequence of the 3 billion chemical base pairs that make up human DNA. This has indeed been an astonishing international undertaking, possibly the largest in modern science, and its findings have already had major implications for understanding the genetic composition of our (and other) species, and determining the place of human beings in the natural environment. Although completed in 2003, interpretation of the data is ongoing and is expected to have a profound effect on medical and biotechnological advances. For example, one of the things that has been slowing down genetic engineering is the fact that geneticists need to identify which specific gene is responsible for traits such as susceptibility to breast cancer, cystic fibrosis or liver disease. The Human Genome Project will provide that information and make it universally available through mapping and databases. One US geneticist, Craig Venter, has already used genomic information to create artificial DNA, a new form of bacteria, and other genetic breakthroughs are sure to follow.

The danger, of course, is that the information may be used for ethically unacceptable purposes. A baby could be genetically coded to conform to standards determined by an elite group with an agenda: to have white skin, for example, or to have an exceptionally high IQ. Venter's discovery could lead to horrific new forms of biological hazards and warfare.

Dyson's third prediction, that the Internet will be a major focus of technological advance in this century, has already proven to be accurate. The Internet was first conceived in 1963 by the Advanced Research Project Agency (ARPA), a division of the US Defense Department, as a means of linking together an array of military computers, so that in the event of a nuclear attack by the Soviet Union, users could communicate with one another regardless of where they were located. Not everyone had to be in the same building. Using a modulator-demodulator, or modem, which converted data into telephone signals, messages were broken down into "packets" and each packet sent through different telephone lines to a given destination. If one line became inoperable (if, say, a nuclear bomb fell on it), its packet would be rerouted through a different line and still arrive at the destination, where all the packets would be reassembled into the original message. This network, called ARPANET, was launched in 1969 between its first two stations, one at the University of California's School of Engineering and Applied Science in Los Angeles, and the other at SRI International, in Menlo Park, also in California. When ARPANET was demilitarized in the 1970s, it was renamed the Internet.

The growth of users of this new system was slow at the start, when it was regarded primarily as an academic tool. But it soared to 100 percent per year throughout the 1990s, after Europe introduced the World Wide Web (WWW) Project, which joined hypertext with the

Internet to allow researchers to share and update information using a Web browser. The WWW was invented by English scientist Tim Berners-Lee (now Sir Timothy Berners-Lee), who at the time was a physicist at CERN, the world's largest particle physics laboratory, located in Geneva, Switzerland. The WWW is essentially a searchable Internet, which means that all information stored on the Internet became accessible to the general public. Suddenly, we were living in an information universe. In June 2009, there were 1.67 billion users on the Internet worldwide.

"The Net, I guarantee you, really is fire," wrote Bran Ferren, the chief Disney Imagineer, in 1997. "I think it's more important than the invention of movable type."[13]

The number of Internet users worldwide is growing at a phenomenal rate. In fact, Dyson may have underestimated the degree to which the Internet has become a universal technology. He foresaw "a clash" between the economic forces driving the technology and the needs of the poor. "The people who are wired, the people who browse the World Wide Web and conduct their daily lives and businesses on the Internet, have tremendous economic and social advantages." And he saw the gulf "between the wired and the unwired" to be growing ever wider.[14]

This doesn't seem to have happened with the Internet. While it's true that, on average, only 25 percent of global citizens are wired, where the Internet is available it is used by people of all social levels, not just the rich. "Modern technology," Ben Seligman wrote in 1966, "is clearly a phenomenon of Western culture."[15] By and large that is still true: 52 percent of Europeans and 74 percent of North Americans are registered Internet users. But the rest of the world is catching up fast. Although only 6.8 percent of Africans use the Internet, that number has increased by 1400 percent since 2000 and it continues to rise. Internet use in Asia, currently around 20 percent, has increased by 545 percent in the past decade. Because of economies of scale, the price of computer hardware has come down almost as fast as the capabilities of computer software have increased. Much software is free, downloadable and sharable, with free Internet access common in libraries, schools, many coffee shops and even some entire cities.

Dyson celebrates the potential of the Internet to improve social conditions for many people. The instantaneous availability of medical information to doctors in remote parts of the world is only one example; the use of satellite email by victims of the January 2010 earthquake in Haiti to alert rescuers of their location under collapsed buildings is another. When Haiti's undersea fiber-optic cable was severed by the quake, rescue agencies were able to keep in touch with one another by satellite.

But the proliferation of electronic technologies is not without its price in the erosion of basic human rights, such as the right to privacy. Since the advent of the World Wide Web, control-related computer technology around the world monitors our workplaces and our private lives. With innovations such as bonus or reward points for purchases, under the guise of giving us discounts in our purchasing, corporations monitor where we shop, what we buy, when we buy it, how much we are willing to pay for it, and even where we store it when we bring it home. This information is then used for such purposes as to fix prices, to direct advertising to the most effective area of a city, and even to keep track of our individual movements as we travel. Electronic readers, now widely available worldwide, are another way in which companies can keep track of consumer trends. It is even conceivable that electronic readers could become an effective tool for government censorship. In July 2009, when Amazon realized it had sold illegally digitized versions of two novels (ironically, both by George Orwell: *Animal Farm* and *Nineteen Eighty-Four*) to customers with electronic readers, the company simply deleted the novels from those devices. No one had known Amazon could do that. It didn't take long for people to realize that similar deletions could be made by anyone who did not wish the public to read certain electronically published material. It isn't only conspiracy theorists who regard cell phones, Air Miles and Kindles as control-related technologies.

There is no doubt that technology has given us huge actual benefits: people living in technologically advanced parts of the world live longer, healthier and easier lives than people living in less "developed" nations. Technology has so changed the way we relate to our environment that it has altered the balance of power between nations. In *Dark Age Ahead*, Jane Jacobs notes that, until about the sixteenth century, the empire builders were the "societies most successful at feeding their people from arable land, pastures, orchards, and gardens." Since then, she writes, "human knowledge and skills, and opportunities to use them, have created postagrarian societies," and it is these new societies, relying on human ingenuity and technology, that have become the "cultural winners." As a result, she writes, history has tended to be seen as irrelevant.[16] Since the Industrial Revolution, postagrarian societies have no longer looked back to the past for inspiration, but forward to the future. Evolution looks back; revolution looks forward.

It is our love affair with progress, and our equating of progress with technology that has made the past seem irrelevant: the past had less (or slower) technology, we think, and was therefore primitive. But technology may be controlling what we remember of the past, filtering out the human. In an essay called "Memoria Ex Machina," American writer Marshall Jon Fisher finds he can remember the Seiko watch he had when he was thirteen, but not "the timbre or inflection of my sister's voice from that time." He recalls lying in bed listening to his clock radio, but not "what time I went to bed as an adolescent, or anything else about my nocturnal ritual." He remembers the technology of his youth, but not his youth itself. "What does it mean," he asks, "that some of my fondest memories are of technology? Have we begun our slide toward the ineluctable merging of man and machine?"[17]

Fisher's fears are not unfounded; they are shared by

many scientists and historians. John Livingston, in *Rogue Primate*, equates technology with civilization and writes that "human domestication is, nearly enough, a synonym for civilization."[18] We have become a domesticated species, tamed by technology and maintained by a world-wide web of technological systems. Historian Daniel Boorstein wrote that "in the world of technology we discover to our horror that we are not so much masters as victims," and that technology "seems to be a law unto itself."[19] Technological revolutions, unlike social or political revolutions, are not reactions to the past, but arise from glimpses of some possible rosy future. They are "reckless," because they obey only their own laws and force us to obey them as well.

Boorstein gives the atomic bomb as an example. The Manhattan Project began as a concerted effort to create an atomic weapon to defeat Germany during the Second World War. Germany was defeated long before the bomb was finished — and yet the technicians went on to complete and deploy the bomb anyway. Technology didn't come to a halt when there was no longer a need for it: technology surged ahead, and then we looked around for a need it could fulfill. Ellen Purdy, director of the Pentagon's Joint Ground Robotics Enterprise, said in 2009 that "we now have a lot of technology, but we don't really know the best way to employ it."[20] This is a scary thought.

The twenty-first-century version of the atomic bomb may be in the field of genetics. Dolly was a clone developed in 1996 from a female sheep that was a perfect specimen of her breed. Geneticists have since cloned a number of domestic and wild animals, mostly for commercial purposes, from a trophy white-tailed deer on a game farm to a favorite cat that had died. The cloning process is expensive and extremely difficult: about one-quarter of all cloned animals have serious health problems, and many die at birth. The cloning of humans is possible, but there are strong ethical arguments against it. For example, who gets to choose the "perfect" human to be cloned? The June 2010 issue of *Scientific American* magazine cites another: "Could people be cloned without their knowledge or consent?" And yet, the magazine's editors deem human cloning to be "inevitable" by the year 2050.[21] Once again, technological progress, like biological evolution, seems irreversible.

But technological progress — the idea that the more technology we get, the better we become — only *seems* like evolution. In fact, the two processes are quite different. We link them because for hundreds of years — since René Descartes and his eighteenth-century followers — we have thought of the biological body as a technological machine. When we think in terms of technology, we make obvious but inaccurate parallels between body parts and machine parts: the mind as a computer, the heart as a pump, the legs like pistons, and so on. Contemporary studies suggest that it is otherwise. The various elements of the body, the very genes that work together to form the proteins and amino acids of our DNA, may function more like thought than like machines. According to British biologist Brian Goodwin, "to make sense of the complexity of gene activity in development, the prevailing model of local mechanical causality will have to be abandoned. In its place, we will have a model of interactive relationships within gene transcription networks, like the pattern of interactions between words in a language."[22] The various elements that combine to make life, he suggests, relate to each other not like gears and weights in a mechanical clock but rather like the words in this paragraph.

In other words, we are not the machine; technology is the machine. We may be servants of the machine, but that is something we can change. One way to do that is rather than make ourselves more like machines, make machines more like us. "The twenty-first century will mark a sea change in human affairs," writes Robert Frenay in *Pulse: The Coming Age of Systems and Machines Inspired by Living Things*, his book about the new biology. "Soon to come are computers with emotions, ships that learn from fish, and 'soft jets' that flex and twist like swooping birds."[23]

Frenay cites nanotechnology as an example of the potential of the new biology, which is sometimes referred to as Biology 2.0.[24] We have already seen that so far nanotechnology has given us little but amusing gadgets — self-cleaning windows, stain-resistant pants. But nanotechnologists envision using microscopic nano-robots that will disassemble materials into their basic building blocks — atoms — and reassemble them into any kind of material we want. Nano-assemblers, for example, could capture carbon atoms from carbon-dioxide emissions and use them to make construction materials that are 100 times stronger than steel and one-sixth the weight. As an added bonus, they would be reducing the amount of carbon entering Earth's atmosphere causing global climate change. Reconstructed "smart molecules" can be embedded in structural material that will allow buildings to change in response to various stimuli: walls could grow thicker in winter and thinner in summer. Frenay quotes a senior advisor to the US National Science Foundation, who says, "Because of nanotechnology, we will see more change in our civilization in the next thirty years than we did during all of the twentieth century."[25]

But more change means faster change, and it is rapid change that has caused the environmental problems we as a civilization are facing today. It is true, for example, that global warming has taken place on Earth before, but in the past the warming of the planet on the scale we are experiencing today has been spread out over hundreds of thousands of years, giving plants and animals plenty of time to adapt and evolve to meet the challenges of new climatic conditions. Our current global warming episode, on the other hand, has taken place in just 250 years, since the rise of coal- and oil-dependent technologies beginning with the Industrial Revolution. Instead of adapting, species are dying out at a rate that hasn't happened since a ten-kilometer-wide (six-mile-wide) meteorite wiped out the dinosaurs, along with 90 percent of all life on Earth, ending the Cretaceous Period of geological history. Technology is having the same impact on Earth that that meteorite had 65 million years ago. In relying on technology to save us from that impact, we're like dinosaurs hoping that the meteorite will miss us. Like meteorites, technology obeys its own laws.

During much of the summer of 2010, oil spewed from a 2000-meter (2187-yard) hole in the floor of the Gulf of Mexico at the rate of 60,000 barrels a day — the equivalent of an *Exxon Valdez* spill every four days. This outpouring from British Petroleum's ruptured Deepwater Horizon oil well represented a significant proportion of the last remaining oil reserves on the planet. Deepwater Horizon is being called the worst environmental disaster in human history. The damage it has caused to wildlife, fisheries and coastal communities is exponentially greater than that caused in 2005, when Hurricane Katrina ruptured the pipelines from oil wells closer to shore, and then president George Bush asked us to be patient while technology found a way to rescue us. Whereas the earlier problem was caused by a natural phenomenon — a hurricane — this current disaster is the direct result of a failure of technology.

When nature caused a problem, we called on technology to save us. But upon whom do we call when it is technology itself that has failed?

Technology Timeline

The exact year of an invention is difficult to pinpoint. A device may be built in one year and patented in another; two or three inventors may lay claim to a certain device; or a date may be assigned based on when an invention was first mentioned in a text or painted on a vase. The following are the generally accepted dates for the inventions that have changed the course of our lives, but other sources may give slightly different accounts.

Date	Technology	Location
2.6 million years ago	Stone tools	Kenya
1.4 million years ago	Fire kit (flint, pyrite)	Kenya
400,000 years ago	Spear	Germany
35,000 years ago	Fish hook	Middle East
	Drill	Egypt
22,000 years ago	Bow and arrow	Europe
20,000 years ago	Boomerang	Carpathian Mountains, Poland
15,000 years ago	Atlatl (throwing stick)	Europe
12,000 years ago	Clay pots (fire baked)	Kyusu Island, Japan
11,000 years ago	Clay pots (sun baked)	Iran
10,000 years ago	Domesticated crops	Fertile Crescent (Middle East)
9,500 years ago	Dugout canoe	Northern Europe
9,000 years ago	Sledge	European arctic regions

9,000 years ago	Shoe	North America
8,000 years ago	Ax	New Guinea
7,500 years ago	Scratch plow	Mesopotamia
5,500 years ago	Wheel (potter's)	Mesopotamia
	Plywood	Egypt
	Sail (square-rigged)	Egypt
5,200 years ago	Wheeled sledge	Mesopotamia
5,000 years ago	Button	Egypt/Mesopotamia
	Ice skates	Finland
	Skis	Lapland
4,800 years ago	Chair	Egypt
4,500 years ago	Bellows	Mesopotamia
	Flush toilet	Indus Valley
	Ink	China
4,000 years ago	Saw	Egypt
3,600 years ago	Rubber ball	Mesoamerica
3,500 years ago	Sundial	Egypt
	Lever	Egypt
	Steel	East Africa
750 BC	Pulley	Assyria
640 BC	Lens	Nineveh (Iraq)
550 BC	Crossbow	China
400 BC	Magnetic compass	China
	Blast furnace	China
300 BC	Stirrup	China
200 BC	Windmill	China
150 BC	Parchment	Turkey

100 BC	Watermill	Greece
AD 79	Claw hammer	Rome
100	Horseshoe	Rome
105	Paper	China
580	Quill pen	Spain
800	Gunpowder	China
984	Canal lock	China
994	Sextant	Iran
999	Mechanical clock	France
1041	Moveable type	China
1180	Vertical windmill	Yorkshire, England
1206	Crankshaft	Syria/Iraq
1300	Musket	China
1320	Production line	Venice
1450	Printing press	Germany
1508	Pocket watch	Germany
1560	Condom	Italy
1589	Knitting frame	England
1609	Telescope	The Netherlands
1614	Cigarettes	Spain
1620	Submarine	Germany
1623	Calculator	Germany
1643	Barometer	Italy
1656	Pendulum clock	The Netherlands

1698	Steam pump	England
1733	Baby carriage	England
1760	Machine-made screws	England
1764	Spinning jenny	England
1765	Steam engine condenser	England
1769	Water frame	England
1776	Steamboat	France
1783	Hot air balloon	France
1784	Bifocals	United States (US)
	Threshing machine	Scotland
1785	Powered loom	England
1791	Gas turbine	England
1793	Cotton gin	US
1795	Hydraulic press	England
1798	Lithographic press	Austria
1799	Battery	Italy
1802	Powdered milk	Russia
1804	Steam locomotive	England
1808	Band saw	England
1810	Tin can	England
1815	Bicycle	Germany
1820	Electromagnet	Denmark
1821	Electric motor	England
1826	Photograph	France

1830	Electromagnetic telegraph	Germany
	Sewing machine	France
1831	Reaper	US
	Dynamo	England
1834	Combine harvester	US
1835	Incandescent light bulb	Scotland
	Revolver	US
1837	Steel plow	US
1838	Newsprint	Canada
1839	Daguerreotype	France
1842	Electric car	US/Scotland
	Analog computer	England
1843	Typewriter	England
1845	Pneumatic tire	England
1846	Rotary printing press	US
1850	Oil refinery	England
1852	Airship	France
Elevator	US	
1859	Rechargeable battery	France
	Spectrometer	Germany
	Internal combustion engine	Belgium
1864	Torpedo	Austria
1866	Dynamite	Sweden
	Electric generator	Belgium
1874	Electric tram	US
	Electric light bulb	Canada

1876	Four-stroke engine	Germany
	Telephone	US
1877	Loudspeaker	Germany
	Phonograph	US
1879	Standard time	Canada
1880	Mousetrap	US
1882	Public electricity supply	US
1884	Linotype printer	Germany
	Photovoltaic cell	US
1885	Motorcycle	Germany
1886	Motorcar	Germany
1887	Contact lens	Germany
1888	Ballpoint pen	US
	Vending machine	US
	Celluloid	US
1889	Brassiere	France
	Juke box	US
	Photographic film	US
1891	Wireless radio	US
1895	Diesel engine	France
	Cinema camera/projector	France
	X-ray photography	Germany
1898	Magnetic recording	Denmark
1901	Assembly line	US
	Electric vacuum cleaner	England
1902	Air conditioner	US

1903	Powered airplane	US
1908	Washing machine	US
	Hydrofoil boat	Canada
1909	Bakelite (plastic)	Belgium
1910	Neon lamp	France
1913	Zipper	US
1921	Lie detector	US
1922	Refrigerator	Sweden
	Technicolor	US
1923	Film sound	US
1926	Television	US
1928	Color television	US
	Cardiac pacemaker	Australia
1929	Coaxial cable	US
1931	Electric guitar	US
	Electron microscope	US
1935	Radar	England
1937	Biodiesel fuel	Belgium
	Jet engine	England/Germany
	Digital computer	US
1938	Ballistic missile	Germany
1939	Helicopter	England
1943	Aqualung	France
1945	Atomic bomb	US
	Microwave oven	US
1947	Transistor	US

1948	Robot	US
1950	Credit card	US
1951	Nuclear reactor	US
1952	Fiber optics	India/England
1956	Hard disc drive	US
	Videotape recording	US
1957	Satellite	USSR
1958	Magnetic swipe card	US
1959	Integrated circuit	US
1960	Laser	US
1963	Artificial heart	US
1968	Computer mouse	US
	Hypertext	US
	Liquid crystal display	US
	IMAX cinematography	Canada
1969	Internet	US
1970	Cellular phone	US
1971	Food processor	France
	Magnetic Resonance Imaging (MRI)	US
	CAT Scan	England
	E-mail	US
1974	Hybrid car	US
1981	"Cyberspace"	Canada
1985	Digital camera	US

1986	Prozac	US/Belgium
	Palmtop computer	England
1987	Bioengineered tissue	US
1988	Digital Subscriber Line (DSL)	US
	Touchpad	US
1989	MP3 player	Germany
	World Wide Web (WWW)	Switzerland
1990	Modem	US
1991	Webcam	England
	Digital cellular phone	Finland
1993	Global Positioning System	US
1995	DVD	US
2001	Satellite radio	US
2007	iPhone	US
2008	Large Hadron Collider	Switzerland/France
2009	Fuel-cell bus	Canada
2010	Artificial DNA	US

Notes

1 Technology and Us

1. The former president was nothing if not consistent. For an earlier version of this sentiment, see Peter North, "Can Economic Growth Save the Environment?" in *Pacific Ecologist* Vol. 9 (Spring 2004), who quotes George W. Bush: "[E]conomic growth is the solution, not the problem. Because a nation that grows its economy can afford investment in new technologies."

2. C.E. Ayres, *The Theory of Economic Progress* (Chapel Hill: University of North Carolina Press, 1944), 105.

3. See Graeme Gibson's introduction to *The Bedside Book of Beasts* (Toronto: Doubleday Canada, 2010). Gibson goes on to say that, since killing at a distance allowed human beings to remove themselves from direct involvement with nature, this was also the beginning of our domestication as a species. See also John Livingston, *Rogue Primate: An Exploration of Human Domestication* (Toronto: General Publishing, 1994).

4. Ursula M. Franklin, *The Real World of Technology* (Toronto: House of Anansi Press, Revised Edition, 1999). Originally given as the CBC Massey Lectures in 1989.

5. Quoted in Gibson, *The Bedside Book of Beasts*, Introduction.

6. Cited by Lewis Mumford in *The Myth of the Machine,* Vol. 2, *The Pentagon of Power* (New York: Harcourt Brace Jovanovich, 1970), 204. Buckminster Fuller was one of the leading American architects of his day, known for championing technological solutions to human problems.

7. Mumford, *The Pentagon of Power*, 204-205.

8. Thomas Carlyle, "Signs of the Times," first published in *The Edinburgh Review* No. 98, 1829. The passage applies so well

to our own age that it is worth quoting in full: "Were we required to characterize this age of ours by any single epithet, we should be tempted to call it, not an Heroical, Devotional, Philosophical, or Moral Age, but, above all others, the Mechanical Age. It is the Age of Machinery."

9. Jack London, *The Iron Heel* (London: Macmillan, 1908), 43.

10. Franklin, *The Real World of Technology*, 19.

11. Gregory J.E. Rawlins, *Slaves of the Machine: The Quickening of Computer Technology* (Cambridge: The MIT Press, 1997), 3.

12. Freeman Dyson, *The Sun, the Genome, and the Internet* (New York: New York Public Library/Oxford University Press, 1999), 61.

13. Chris Hedges, *Empire of Illusion: The End of Literacy and the Triumph of Spectacle* (Toronto: Alfred A. Knopf, 2009), 142.

14. Aldous Huxley, "The Outlook for American Culture," *Harper's Magazine*, August 1927.

15. Martin L. van Creveld, *Technology and War: From 2000 BC to the Present* (New York: Free Press, 1988), 5.

16. Cited by Stephen R. Bown in *A Most Damnable Invention: Dynamite, Nitrates, and the Making of the Modern World* (New York: Thomas Dunne Books, 2005), 15.

17. Quoted in Bown, *A Most Damnable Invention*, 114.

18. Mumford, *The Pentagon of Power*, 258-72.

19. J.M. Coetzee, *Diary of a Bad Year* (New York: Penguin, 2008), 48. Although a novel, *Diary of a Bad Year* is made up in part of a series of nonfiction essays, from which this description is taken.

20. I heard Carol Graham on a radio interview. She was promoting her book, *Happiness Around the World: The Paradox of*

Happy Peasants and Miserable Millionaires (Oxford and New York: Oxford University Press, 2010).

2 Technology and the Control of Nature

1. Franklin, *The Real World of Technology*, 9.
2. Lewis Mumford, "The First Megamachine," *Diogenes* No. 55 (Fall 1966), 1-5. Reprinted in Donald L. Miller, ed., *The Lewis Mumford Reader* (New York: Pantheon Books, 1986), 315-20.
3. Adrian Goldsworthy, *The Fall of the West: The Slow Death of the Roman Superpower* (London: Phoenix Books, 2010), 40 ff.
4. Wilkie Collins, *The Woman in White, 1859-60*. The quote is from the Penguin Classics edition (Harmondsworth, 1985), 34.
5. Mumford, *The Pentagon of Power*, 425.
6. St. John Chrysostom, *Epistle to the Ephesians*, Homily XXII, 2.
7. David F. Noble, *The Religion of Technology: The Divinity of Man and the Spirit of Invention* (New York: Alfred A. Knopf, 1997), 4-5.
8. See Mumford's essay "The Monastery and the Clock," in *The Lewis Mumford Reader*, 333-47.

3 The Renaissance

1. Quoted in Friedrich Klemm, *A History of Western Technology* (Cambridge: The MIT Press, 1959), 112.
2. Ironically, it was Evelyn who first proposed to the "natural philosopher" Robert Boyle the formation of England's Royal Society, a group of scientists and inventors whose aim was "to improve practical and experimental knowledge"; in other words, to translate scientific theories into technological realities. See Noble, *The Religion of Technology*, 58-69.

3. John Man, *The Gutenberg Revolution: The Story of a Genius and an Invention that Changed the World* (London: Review, 2002), 261-83.

4. Mumford, *The Pentagon of Power*, 138.

5. Carlyle, "Signs of the Times."

6. Wade Davis, *The Wayfinders* (Toronto: House of Anansi Press, 2009), 120.

7. Klemm, *A History of Western Technology*, 140.

4 The Industrial Revolution

1. Watts's patent application is reproduced in Klemm, *A History of Western Technology*, 256-259.

2. William Woodruff, *Impact of Western Man: A Study of Europe's Role in the World Economy 1750-1960* (New York: St. Martin's Press, 1966), 1.

3. Gavin Menzes, *1434: The Year a Magnificent Chinese Fleet Sailed to Italy and Ignited the Renaissance* (New York: Harper Perennial, 2009). The Chinese had had the compass for centuries, but theirs pointed south rather than north, and was used originally for divination, not navigation.

4. Alan Lightman, *A Sense of the Mysterious: Science and the Human Spirit* (New York: Pantheon Books, 2005), 194.

5. Voltaire was particularly enamored of canals. In his *Siecle de Louis XIV*, he enthuses over the Languedoc Canal, which opened in 1681, as the Sun King's greatest accomplishment: "his most glorious monument for its utility, its grandeur, and its difficulties." Cited by A. W. Skempton, "Canal and River Navigations before 1750," in *A History of Technology*, Volume III, Charles Singer et. al., eds. (Oxford: The Clarendon Press,

1957), 466. Jacques Elul, in *The Technological Society* (New York: Vintage Books, 1964), 46, notes "the philosophy of the eighteenth century did indeed favor technical applications. It was naturalistic and sought not only to know but also to exploit nature."

6. Andrew Ure, *The Philosophy of Manufactures: or, An Exposition of the Scientific, Moral, and Commercial Economy of the Factory System of Great Britain* (London: Charles Knight, 1835), 21.

7. Lightman, *A Sense of the Mysterious*: "By inner self I mean that part of me that imagines, that dreams, that explores, that is constantly questioning who I am and what is important to me. My inner self is my true freedom."

8. Carlyle, "Signs of the Times."

9. Kirkpatrick Sale, "Lessons from the Luddites," *The Ecologist* No. 29, August 5, 1999.

10. Louis-René Villermé, *Study of the Physical Condition of Cotton, Wool and Silk Workers*, 1840, 3.

11. Ure maintained that children were more often abused by their parents than by mill owners. Children were employed by the spinner, not by the mill owner, and if any beating was done, it was done by the spinner. "Often [the children] were the spinner's own off-spring or relations" (301). See also Arthur Redford, *Labour Migration in England, 1800-1850* (London: Clarendon Press, 1926), 51: "[A]s the Factory Act of 1833 prevented handloom weavers from sending their young children into the factories, many sent them into the mines."

12. Both comments by Robert Southey are quoted in Andrew Ure, *The Philosophy of Manufactures* (London: Charles Knight, Ludgate-Street, 1835), 277-78.

13. Jacob Bigelow, *Elements of Technology* (Boston: Hilliard, Gray, Little, and Wilkins, 1829), 3. Although Bigelow's allusion to cheap means of gratifying our wants sounds like a criticism of technology, the phrase was meant to indicate a positive advance in civilization from "complete barbarism" to "perfect refinement."

14. Louise Purbrick, ed., *The Great Exhibition of 1851: New Interdisciplinary Essays* (2001), 2. In her introduction, Purbrick notes that the exhibition "illustrated the achievement of industrial technology without reference to the conditions of industrial labour."

15. William Wordsworth's poem, "The World is Too Much With Us," is thought to have been written around 1802 and was first published in 1807.

16. Samuel Butler, *Erewhon* (London: Penguin Books, 1970 [1872]), 206. Butler echoed Andrew Ure's idea that machines had taken on a form of human intelligence: "But who can say that the vapour engine [i.e., the steam engine] has not a kind of consciousness? Where does consciousness begin, and where end? Who can draw the line? Is not everything interwoven with everything?", 199.

5 Modern Times

1. *Harper's Magazine*, April 1857, "Editor's Table," 697-98.

2. Perry Miller, "The Responsibility of Mind in a Civilization of Machines," *American Scholar* XXXI (Winter 1961-62), 51.

3. Thomas P. Hughes, *American Genesis: A Century of Invention and Technological Enthusiasm* (New York: Penguin Books, 1989), 6.

4. *Harper's Magazine*, 697.

5. Dyson, *The Sun, the Genome, and the Internet*, 53.

6. Franklin, *The Real World of Technology*, 33.

7. Hughes, *American Genesis*, 188-203.

8. Hughes, *American Genesis*, 185.

9. Barry Commoner, personal communication, 2004.

10. Patricia E. Moody and Richard E. Morley, *The Technology Machine: How Manufacturing Will Work in the Year 2020* (New York: The Free Press, 1999), 14 ff.

11. Moody and Morley, *The Technology Machine*, 14-15.

12. President Barack Obama seems to have agreed with Dyson. One of his first acts as president in 2008 was the withdrawal of a large amount of financial support to NASA and the space program.

13. Bran Ferren, "Society Evolving," in Richard Rhodes, ed., *Visions of Technology: A Century of Vital Debate About Machines, Systems and the Human World* (New York: Simon and Schuster, 1999), 370-71.

14. Dyson, *The Sun, the Genome, and the Internet*, 58.

15. Ben B. Seligman, *Most Notorious Victory: Man in an Age of Automation* (New York: The Free Press, 1966), 4. Seligman goes on to say that "in ancient times, men could control their technology and shape their philosophy by the heavens. The capacity to do that today is moot."

16. Jane Jacobs, *Dark Age Ahead* (Toronto: Random House, 2004), 162-65.

17. Marshall Jon Fisher, "Memoria Ex Machina," in *DoubleTake* (Summer 2002). Reprinted in *Best American Essays 2003*, Anne Fadiman, ed. (Boston: Houghton Mifflin, 2003).

18. John A. Livingston, *Rogue Primate: An Exploration of Human Domestication* (Toronto: Key Porter Books, 1994), 13.

19. Daniel Boorstein, *Hidden History: Exploring Our Secret Past* (New York: Vintage Books, 1987), 236-37.

20. Quoted by Evan Ratliff in "Shoot!", an article about robots and warfare in *The New Yorker*, February 23, 2009, 34.

21. *Scientific American* (June 2010), 36.

22. Brian Goodwin, "The Organism Itself as the Emergent Meaning," in John Brockman, ed., *This Will Change Everything: Ideas That Will Shape the Future* (New York: Harper Perennial, 2010), 333.

23. It should be noted here that the new biology is not all that new. In *Physics and Philosophy*, published in 1942, British physicist Sir James Jeans wrote, "Today there is a wide measure of agreement on the physical side of science approaching almost to unanimity, that the stream of knowledge is heading towards a non-mechanical reality; the universe is beginning to look more like a great thought than like a great machine."

24. Robert Frenay, *Pulse: The Coming Age of Systems and Machines Inspired by Living Things* (New York: Farrar, Straus and Giroux, 2006), 4.

25. Frenay, *Pulse*, 46. The senior advisor's name was Mike Roco.

For Further Information

Brockman, John, ed. *This Will Change Everything: Ideas That Will Shape the Future.* New York: Harper Perennial, 2010.

Dibbell, Jillian, ed. *The Best Technology Writing 2010.* New Haven: Yale University Press, 2010.

Ellul, Jacques. *The Technological Society.* New York: Alfred A. Knopf, 1964.

Franklin, Ursula M. *The Real World of Technology.* Toronto: House of Anansi Press, 1989. Revised Edition, 1999.

Frenay, Robert. *Pulse: The Coming Age of Systems and Machines Inspired by Living Things.* New York: Farrar, Straus and Giroux, 2006.

Grady, Wayne. *Bringing Back the Dodo: Lessons in Natural and Unnatural History.* Toronto: McClelland and Stewart, 2006.

Grant, George. *Technology and Empire.* Toronto: House of Anansi Press, 1969.

Hughes, Thomas P. *American Genesis: A Century of Invention and Technological Enthusiasm.* New York: Penguin Books, 1989.

Lanier, Jaron. *You Are Not a Gadget: A Manifesto.* London: Allan Lane, 2010.

Livingston, John. *Rogue Primate: An Exploration of Human Domestication.* Toronto: Key Porter Books, 1994.

Mander, Jerry. *Four Arguments for the Elimination of Television.* New York: Quill, 1977, 1978.

McKibben, Bill. *Enough: Staying Human in an Engineered Age.* New York: Henry Holt and Company, 2003.

Mumford, Lewis. *The Myth of the Machine*, Vol. 2, *The Pentagon of Power.* New York: Harcourt Brace Jovanovich, 1970.

Rutsky, R. L. *High Techne: Art and Technology from the Machine Aesthetic to the Posthuman*. Minneapolis: University of Minnesota Press, 1999.

Seligman, Ben B. *Most Notorious Victory: Man in an Age of Automation*. New York: The Free Press, 1966.

Wright, Ronald. *A Short History of Progress*. Toronto: House of Anansi Press, 2004.

Acknowledgments

Everyone feels strongly about technology, whether for or against. My neighbor covers her ears when I try to explain how to search Craigslist, as though deafness will stem the advancing tide, and my friend Ross Laird, who believes we have entered a new phase of human evolution, speaks so eloquently on the subject that this book is a lot less technophobic than it might have been. Graeme Gibson, friend and now editor of the late John Livingston, and I have sat late into the night, toasting the vagaries of human domestication with elixirs made with tools no more sophisticated than peat knives and spokeshaves. Another late-night, and now late, friend, Matt Cohen, once a protégé of George Grant, also helped me formulate some of the ideas expressed in this book.

I would like to thank Michelle Benjamin, who invited me to contribute to *A Passion for This Earth*, a festschrift for David Suzuki published in 2008 by Greystone Books. My essay for that collection, "The Mechanical Savior," formed the basis for my thoughts on Luddism in modern society. Also instrumental was my essay "Send in the Clones," first published in *Explore* magazine and later in *Bringing Back the Dodo*. An updated version, read at Green College, University of British Columbia, in September 2007, started me thinking about the relationship between technology and religion.

Patsy Aldana, doyen of Groundwood Books, warmed immediately to the idea of a book on technology and was supportive throughout. Jane Springer helped shape a lot of rambling incohesion into an actual book. And Nan Froman, as always, kept the stylistic locomotive safely on its track. I extend my lasting gratitude to my agent, Bella Pomer. And also to my wife, Merilyn Simonds, who never fails to inspire and nurture.

Index

Note: A page reference containing "n" refers to the Notes section. For example, 130n4:5 means page 130, chapter 4, note 5.